# Horse Antiques
# & Collectibles

Deborah Rashkin

Schiffer Publishing Ltd®

4880 Lower Valley Road, Atglen, PA 19310 USA

# *Dedication*

Illustration from the *Sportsman's Sketchbook* by Lionel Edwards RI, "Sea Bathing."

With love to my family, Stan, Ashley, Ben and Andrew, and in loving memory of my mother Arquita C. McCleary.

"Give to me nutritious food:
Give me water pure and good:
When the chilling winds do blow,
Over me a blanket throw:
Shield me from all cruelty:
When I'm old be kind to me."

Harriet Biggle, c.1910

*Title page:* Victorian style print of a boy and girl with white pony, printed on vellum, Germany, c. 1905. 21" h. x 16" w. $70-95.

Copyright © 2001 by Deborah Rashkin
Library of Congress Card Number: 2001089208

Designed by Bonnie M. Hensley
Cover design by Bruce M. Waters
Type set in Cataneo BT/Zapf Humanist BT

ISBN: 0-7643-1350-9
Printed in China
1 2 3 4

Published by Schiffer Publishing Ltd.
4880 Lower Valley Road
Atglen, PA 19310
Phone: (610) 593-1777; Fax: (610) 593-2002
E-mail: Schifferbk@aol.com
Please visit our web site catalog at
**www.schifferbooks.com**

This book may be purchased from the publisher.
Include $3.95 for shipping. Please try your bookstore first.
We are always looking for people to write books on new and related subjects. If you have an idea for a book please contact us at the above address.
You may write for a free catalog.

In Europe, Schiffer books are distributed by
Bushwood Books
6 Marksbury Avenue
Kew Gardens
Surrey TW9 4JF England
Phone: 44 (0) 20-8392-8585; Fax: 44 (0) 20-8392-9876
E-mail: Bushwd@aol.com
Free postage in the UK. Europe: air mail at cost.

# Acknowledgements

I would like to personally thank the many people that I have had contact with during the preparation and writing of this book. I sincerely appreciate the time, knowledge and encouragement that you have shared with me. To my good friend Amelia Yeager, I extend a very special thank you for your support, enthusiasm, and tireless contribution to making this book a reality.

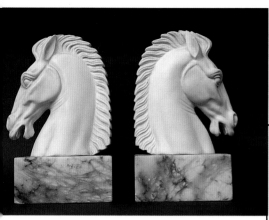

vorine horse head bookends on marble base,
c. 1950. 8.25" h. x 5.75" w. $275+.

Print of Edward Herber Miner
painting, taken from *National
Geographic, World of Horses,*
c. November, 1923. 10" h. x 7" w.
$45-75.

# *Contents*

# Introduction to Collecting

Exquisite pewter lamp with white glass globe, elegant deco horse head design, c. 1920. 27" h. x 7.75" w. $350+.

Collectors, much like horse people, are passionate. Just as one would not (or should not) buy a horse without first giving it some thought, much the same can be said for collecting. I have composed a list of suggestions that I hope you will find helpful.

I like to think of collecting in terms of going on a treasure hunt—you can never be quite sure what your adventure will uncover. Be resourceful in your search and explore all areas, from garage sales and flea markets to local shops and super malls, antique shows, clubs and associations, and of course, cyberspace. Each avenue presents exciting opportunities for exploration.

Whenever possible, handle a piece; examine its texture, composition, and markings. If you have a question, now is the time to ask. A wealth of information is available from knowledgeable professionals who can impart details and facts that you might otherwise never have known. Establishing the provenance of a piece only adds to its value.

Also, be aware that many well-crafted reproductions exist in the marketplace. If in doubt, I again encourage you to seek the advice of someone with expertise in the area in which you are looking.

When determining value, the true rule of thumb is that a particular piece is worth what the market will bear. However, it is also important to take other factors into consideration, such as location, condition, rarity, current trends, and desirability. All of the preceding play a role in constituting the value of a specific item.

Lastly—but to me most importantly—collect or purchase items that you truly like. Chances are the piece comes with a cherished past and now it is *your* chance to have, share, and add on to that unique history.

## Author's Note

Pieces presented in this book are the property of the author. Photographs in this book were taken by, and/or are the property of the author. Circa refers to an era, it does not determine a specific date unless it is stated as one. The value ranges stated in this book are retail values for items in good to excellent condition. While the author has endeavored to estimate current market values, neither the author nor the publisher are responsible for the accuracy of the values stated herein and recommend that they be used as a guide only.

Standing foal single bookend, Champion Products, "PHILLIPE DI NAPOLI" (artist), c. 1930. 7.25" h. x 6" w. $150-250 pair.

# The Horse: Past and Present

From beast of burden to a beloved and cherished friend, the horse's relationship with man has existed and endured the trials of time. There is something almost magical that draws us to this most noble and majestic of creatures.

Approximately fifty to fifty-five million years ago, *Hyracotherium*, formerly *Eohippus*, first appeared in North America. *Hyracotherium* remained the sole species until about thirty-seven million years ago, when it evolved further to produce at least a dozen other new species in America. It was from these roots that the genus *Equus* sprang. *Equus* was a single-toed mammal, which over time became the horses, ponies, zebras, and other associated relatives of today. After completely disappearing from North America, the horse did not re-emerge again until people from the other side of the Atlantic transported it across the ocean. There are many theories as to why the horse suddenly vanished from North America. One exact reason has never been established, however, and the different theories are debatable. It is known that the horse's disappearance was sudden and occurred approximately ten thousand years ago.

HORSES

COPYRIGHT, 1902, BY DODD, MEAD & COMPANY

JULIUS BIEN & CO. LITH. N.Y.

1 WILD ASS - EQUUS ASINUS
2 BURCHELL'S ZEBRA - EQUUS BURCHELLI
3 HORSE (THOROUGHBRED)
4 DOMESTIC DONKEY

Color lithograph showing four members of the horse family, c. 1902. 5" h. x 8" w. $15-25.

Today we recognize horses from only two species: *Equus ferus*, perhaps better known as Przewalski's horse, and *Equus caballus*, the domesticated horse derived from *Equus ferus*.

It is felt that domestication of the horse began during the third millennium or perhaps even slightly earlier. An historian, general, and revered horseman named Xenophon (430-354 BC) authored a treatise on horses and horsemanship which is still read and held in high acclaim today. He wrote, "If you reward him with kindness when he has done what you wish and admonish him when he disobeys, he will be most likely to do what you want. This holds good in every branch of horsemanship."

Detail of "Halt," colored transfer on white plate, signed, c. mid twentieth century. 9.25" dia. $30-40.

By viewing many cultures in retrospect, we are able to see the roles and influence that the horse portrayed in its development. Literature, art, and history all provide evidence of the horse's revered stature: Paleolithic horse portraits painted in caves of France and Spain, the Egyptian chariot horses portrayed in art of the fourteenth dynasty, the magnificently sculpted Greek and Roman objects d'art, and the recognizable style of the Chinese Tang horse are but a few illustrations from previous eras.

Today, perhaps more than ever before, the horse has transcended from a relationship based on dependency to one of passion. In knowing him we become refreshed and are able to see the uniqueness and beauty that time has only enhanced.

As a final thought I impart the words of Harriet Biggle, who with her wit and wisdom perhaps says it best: "You cannot whip terror out of a horse or pound courage into one. Kindness and reasonable persuasion are the best weapons to use in training and educating a horse. If he shies or frightens, soothe and encourage him, rather than beat and abuse him."

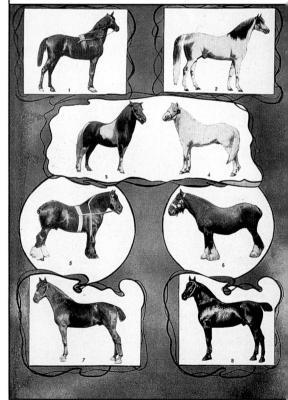

Photo lithograph of eight different breeds of horses, c. 1904. 7" h. x 5" w. $15-25.

# Chapter 1

# Pottery, Porcelain, & Ceramics

> "There is something about the outside of a horse that is good for the inside of a man."
>
> —Sir Winston Churchill (1874-1965)

## Pottery and Ceramic Figures

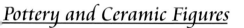

*Top left:* Bay horse figurine, Lefton's, Japan, c. 1953-71. 5.5" h. x 5.5" w. $40-65.

*Center right:* Palomino horse figurine, Lefton's, Japan, c. 1953-71. 5.5" h. x 5.5" w. $40-65.

*Center left:* Black horse figurine, Vcagco, Japan, c. 1950-60. 5.5" h. x 6.5" w. $25-40.

*Bottom right:* Trio of ceramic horses.

White horse head planter, Lefton, Japan, c. 1960-83. 6" h. x 6.25" w. $25-45.

Brown and white horse head planter, Inarco, Japan, c. 1960-present. 5.25" h. x 7" w. $20-35.

Palomino horse head planter, Giftwares Co., Japan, c. 1950-present. 5.25" h. x 6.5" w. $20-35.

Bay horse head planter, Lefton, Japan, c. 1962-90. 6.5" h. x 6.5" w. $25-45.

Ivory horse head planter, Relpo, Chicago, Illinois, Made in Japan, c. 1950-present. 5.75" h. x 6" w. $20-35.

Bay horse head wall plaque, Lefton's, Japan, c. 1953-71. 8.25" h. x 6.5" w. $35-50.

Alabaster horse head wall plaque, Norcrest, Japan, c. 1960. 7.25" h. x 6.25" w. $30-45.

Bay mare and foal planter, Napcoware, Japan, c. 1938-present. 5.5" h. x 4.5" w. $25-40.

Triple horse head planter, Norcrest, Japan, c. 1960. 5.5" h. x 8" w. $35-50.

Bay mare and foal planter, Napcoware, Japan, c. 1938-present. 6.25" h. x 6.75" w. $30-45.

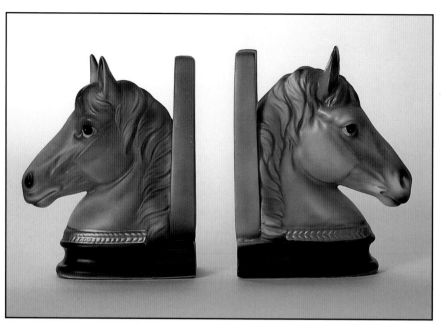

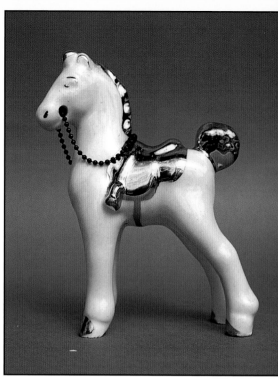

Standing white horse with gold trim, Grindley Pottery, Sebring, Ohio, c. 1933-53. 5.25" h. x 4" w. $25-40.

Palomino horse head bookends, Arnart, Japan, c. second half twentieth century. 6.5" h. x 5" w. $45-70.

Spotted white pony with gold accent, Grindley Artware Manufacturing Co., c. 1933-52. 4.25" h. x 5.5" w. $30-40.

Standing yellow pony accentuated with gold, Grindley Pottery, Sebring, Ohio, c. 1933-53. 5.25" h. x 3.25" w. $20-35.

Pastel trio of ponies, Shawnee Pottery, c. 1937-61. 5.25" h. x 5.5" w. $15-20 each.

Sitting pony planters, American Bisque or Shawnee Pottery, c. 1940-60. 4.5" h. x 6.5" w. $15-25 each.

Standing blue horse with black hooves, Morton Pottery, c. 1950. 6.25" h. x 5.5" w. $20-30.

Green and gray mare and foal planters, American Bisque, c. 1950. 5.5" h. x 5" w. $25-35 each.

Primitive brown and white standing pony, Occupied Japan, c. 1947-52. 3.25" h. x 4.5" w. $10-20.

Black rearing horse salt and pepper set, Japan, c. 1950. 4.5" h. $15-20.

Three whimsical pony figures, Norcrest Exclusive, Japan, c. 1950. Black, 5" h. x 3.5" w. Brown, 4.5" h. x 4" w. Grey, 5" h. x 4.5" w. $20-35 each.

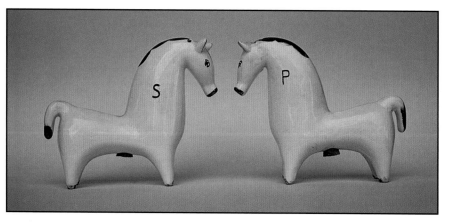

White retro horse salt and pepper shakers, unmarked, c. 1940-50. 4.5" h. x 5.5" w. $20-30.

Large metallic pony planter, Kenwood, U.S.A., c. 1938-58. 8.5" h. x 8" w. $40-60.

Two-toned green deco horse planter, Royal Copley, c. 1939-60. 5.75" h. x 6.75" w. $35-55.

Brown pony on yellow planter, Royal Copley, c. 1939-60. 5.25" h. x 4.75" w. $30-45.

Colorful pony planter, Relpo, Chicago, Illinois, Made in Japan, c. 1950-present. 6" h. x 6" w. $20-30.

Decorative planter with mare watching foal, unmarked, c. 1940-50. 6" h. x 8.5" w. $40-65.

Vintage rearing brown horse on lime green base, Artistic Potteries, California, c. 1940. 13" h. x 10" w. $60-80.

Stylized black and gray horse on green base, Lane & Co., California, c. 1952. 11" h. x 13.5" w. $70-85.

Gray horse with water trough planter, Lane & Co., California, c. 1950. 9.5" h. x 13.5 " w. $50-70.

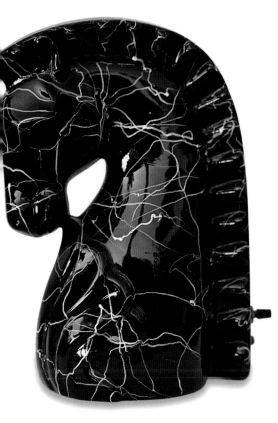

Green rearing horse T.V. lamp, unmarked, c. mid twentieth century. 8.5" h. x 6.5" w. $100-120.

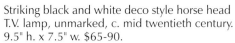

Striking black and white deco style horse head T.V. lamp, unmarked, c. mid twentieth century. 9.5" h. x 7.5" w. $65-90.

Black horse and colt T.V. lamp accented with white, unmarked, c. mid twentieth century. 9" h. x 10.5" w. $75-95.

Prancing brown horse on decorative base T.V. lamp, Lane & Co., California, c. 1939. 9.25" h. x 9" w. $85-110.

Mottled brown horse and foal T.V. lamp and planter, unmarked, c. 1940. 10.75" h. x 11.5" w. $85-100.

Elegant green rearing horse highlighted with 22K gold T.V. lamp, La Mieux China, c. 1940. 14.75" h. x 9" w. $95-110.

Brown ceramic deco style horse head T.V. lamp, unmarked, c. 1940. 10.5" h. x 7.25" w. $65-90.

Green fighting horse T.V. lamp and planter with 22K gold accent, Lampcrafts American China, c. mid twentieth century. 7.5" h. x 9.5" w. $75-90.

Shades of brown double horse head T.V. lamp, unmarked, c. 1940. 8.25" h. x 11" w. $75-95.

Resting brown mare and colt lamp with wooden base, unmarked, c. 1950. 24" h. x 10" w. $90-125.

Red rearing horse lamp and planter with white highlighting, unmarked, c. mid twentieth century. 20" h. x 8.5" w. $60-80.

Detail of brown mare and colt lamp.

Variegated green and tan rearing horse lamp with planters, unmarked, c. 1950. 21" h. x 13" w. $75-95.

Deco style green horse head lamp, unmarked, c. 1940-50. 19" h. x 6" w. $55-75.

Detail of base with planters.

Art deco double horse head in an iridescent black glaze with deep green highlights, unmarked, c. 1930. 20" h. x 6.5" w. $65-85.

Green and brown glazed rearing horse lamp, unmarked, c. 1950. 20" h. x 7" w. $65-85.

Detail of double horse head base.

Red Trojan style horse head lamp, unmarked, c. mid twentieth century. 22" h. x 7" w. $55-75.

Detail of red Trojan style horse head lamp.

# Chalkware

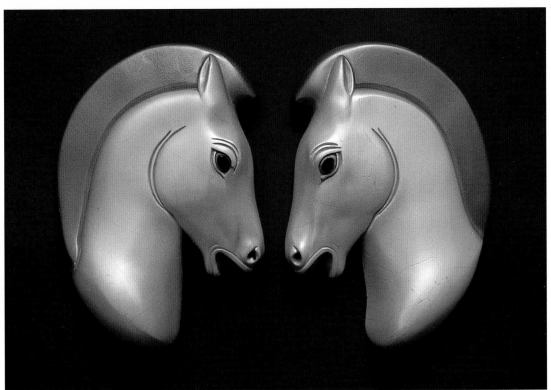

White chalkware horse heads accented with gold mane, unmarked, c. 1950. 8.75" h. x 7.25" w. $30-45 set.

Chalkware wall plaque, white horse head surrounded by gold frame, unmarked, c. 1950. 11" h. x 8" w. $15-25.

Mustang wall plaque, Napco, Japan, c. 1938-present. 5.25" h. x 6.5" w. $20-30.

Thoroughbred wall plaque, Napco, Japan, c. 1938-present. 5" h. x 5" w. $20-30.

Good luck chalkware horseshoe with four leaf clover, unmarked, c. 1940-50. 6.25" h. x 4.5" w. $20-30.

White chalkware carnival horse, air brushed with red and blue, unmarked, c. mid twentieth century. 10" h. x 8" w. $45-65.

Brown chalkware horse on base, unmarked, c. 1950. 6.5" h. x 5.75" w. $20-35.

Chalkware relief of horse head in circular plaque, General Art Co., c. 1950. 7" dia. $25-35.

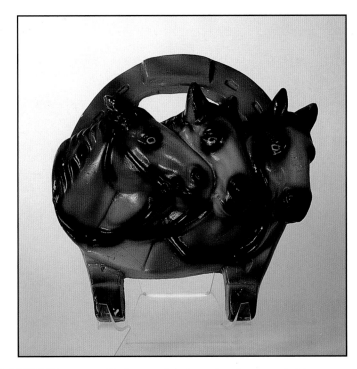

Chalkware double horse head, Miller Studio, Inc., c. 1964. 5.5" h. x 6.5" w. $20-30.

Chalkware triple horse head surrounded by horseshoe, unmarked, c. 1940. 9" dia. $25-40.

Pair of chalkware single horse heads, Miller Studio, Inc., c. 1951. 4" h. x 4.5" w. $15-25 each.

Black chalkware horse head bookends, Alexander Baker Co., New York, c. 1950. 7.5" h. x 6" w. $50-75.

Painted chalkware village scene bookends, unmarked, c. 1946. 5.5" h. x 4.5" w. $50-75.

Chalkware clock, unmarked, clock has Lanshire movement, c. 1940-50. 8" h. x 13.5" w. $75-95.

Chalkware horse head lamp, signed M.A., c. 1950. 29.25" h. $95-120.

Detail of chalkware horse head lamp.

# *Finer Pottery and Porcelain*

Elegant gray horse head vase, Royal Copley, c. 1939-60. 8.25" h. $40-60.

Green multi-colored horse head vase/bookend, Royal Haeger, c. 1938. 8.75" h. $45-65.

Glazed brown horse head vase, Haeger Potteries, Dundee, Illinois, c. 1914-present. 8.25" h. $45-65.

Golden glazed standing horse planter, Haeger U.S.A., c. 1960. 8.75" h. x 7.5" w. $55-75.

Marvelous cocoa colored horse serving platter, California Pottery, c. mid twentieth century. 10" h. x 16.75" w. $65-85.

Detail of California Pottery horse platter.

Two ornate yellow horse figurines, Cemar Clay Products Co., c. 1945-57. Grazing foal, 3" h. x 3.5" w. $35-50. Rearing horse, 6" h. x 5" w. $45-65.

Standing yellow horse on green base, Cemar Clay Products Co., c. 1945-57. 5.85" h. x 4.3" w. $45-65.

Pair of brown and white rearing horses with 22K gold mane and tail, Morton Potteries, c. 1940. 7" h. x 5.25" w. $30-45 pair.

Stylized deco horse planters, Brush McCoy, unmarked, c. 1940. 6.5" h. x 8" w. $45-70.

Dunn colored horse figurine, Goebel, West Germany, c. 1937-45. 4.25" h. x 5.5" w. $65-85.

Outstanding Clydesdale horse, Poppytrail Pottery by Metlox, c. 1940-60. 9" h. x 9" w. $175-185.

Lusterware hunter ashtray with snuffers and horseshoe trays, Made in Japan, c. mid twentieth century. 5.5" h. x 4.5" w. $40-75.

Colorful hand painted miniature porcelain hunter on horse, numbered, Germany, c. 1890-1920. $75-95.

White porcelain horse and rider with gold accent, Erphila, manufactured in Germany for Eberling & Reuss, Pennsylvania, c. 1930-40. 4" h. x 3.75" w. $95-120.

Elegant off-white standing horse on gold base, Royal Dux, Czechoslovakia, c. latter twentieth century. 8.5" h. x 9" w. $175-250.

Glossy black and dusty pink horse head bookends, Abingdon Potteries, c. 1934-50. 6.5" h. x 3.5" w. $55-75.

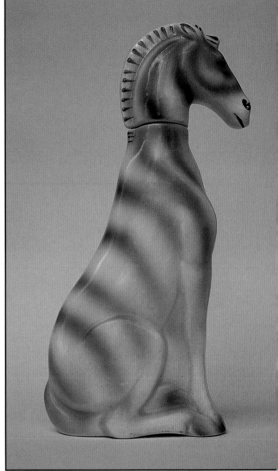

Abstract burgundy horse head embossed with gold, Westwood Ware, California Pottery, c. mid twentieth century. 8" h. x 7.5" w. $50-65.

Unique green and white striped porcelain decanter, "Ardico Products," "E.P.P. & Co.," "Germany," c. 1920-30. 8" h. x 3.5" w. $50-60.

Poised white ceramic horse head bookends, signed, "Champion," c. early to mid twentieth century. 7.75" h. x 5" w. $85-110.

Sophisticated California Pottery horse head pitchers, Artistic Pottery, California, c. 1940. 8.5" h. x 4.5" w. $60-80 each.

Detail of Artistic Pottery horse head pitcher.

Picturesque scene of horses grazing, Three Crown China, Germany, c. early twentieth century. 10.5" dia. $50-70.

Chestnut mare tending foal, Kaiser, W. Germany, c. 1970. 7.75" dia. $30-45.

Austrian Lipizzaner by Susie Whitcombe, Spode, c. 1988. 8.5" dia. $20-35.

Arabian photo on white plate with decorative gold border design, Champion Indroff, Al-Marah Arabian Horse Farm, plate manufactured by Steubenville, c. mid twentieth century. 10" dia. $45-65.

Elegant horse head surrounded by golden wheat on fine porcelain with scalloped edge, C.A. Lehmann and Son, Leuchtenburg, Germany, c. 1910-35. 10" dia. $65-85.

Stunning gray horse head set on brown background edged in gold, H & C, Bavaria, c. 1930-present. 8.5" dia. $45-75.

Detail of H & C, Bavaria plate.

Simplified Arts & Crafts style brass salver, unmarked, c. 1920-30. 10" dia. $40-60.

"Favonius," Epson Downs Derby winner set on white plate banded in gold, Sabin, Crest-O-Gold, c. 1946-79. 7.25" dia. $30-45.

Elegant Flow Blue hunt scene, Royal Doulton, England, c. early twentieth century. 9.5" dia. $90-120.

Detail of hunting scene on Royal Doulton plate.

Ornate cobalt blue plate with hunt scene and gold accents, Victoria, Austria, c. 1904-18. 6" dia. $60-80.

Fisher Gibson Girl and horse calendar plate, unmarked, c. 1910. 8.25" dia. $70-95.

Detail of Fisher Gibson Girl and horse.

Equestrian calendar plate, unmarked, c. 1911. 7.25" dia. $70-95.

Detail of equestrian plate center.

Royal Bayreuth grouping featuring equestrian bowls, farm scene plates, and creamer, Royal Bayreuth, Germany, c. 1890-1920. Plates, 6" dia. $125-175 each. Bowls, 5" dia. $90-120 each. Creamer, 4.5" h. $110-140.

Royal Bayreuth farm scene pipe ashtray, Royal Bayreuth, Germany, c. 1890-1920. 4.25" l. x 3.25" w. $150-200.

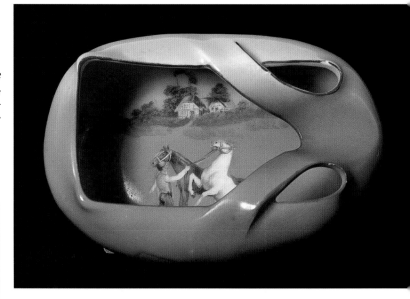

Detail of farm scene plates.

Ridgways plate, scene from Coaching Days series, by special permission of MacMillan Co. Ltd., England, c. early twentieth century. 9" dia. $30-50.

Detail of Ridgways plate, Coaching series, "Taking out the Leaders."

Royal Doulton Coaching Days, loading of the carriage, Royal Doulton, England, c. 1905-55. 8" dia. $65-85.

Royal Doulton Coaching Days, farewell to carriage, Royal Doulton, England, c. 1905-55. 8" dia. $65-85.

*Top left:* German hand painted porcelain plate, equestrian motif with horse and rider, scarlet border with gold leaf trim and foliage, signed: EGRO Wien Porzellan – A. OTTLINGER Sevelen, c. twentieth century. 7.75" dia. $60-80.

*Top right:* Oversize cup with cross country riding couple in pastel tones, Three Crown, Germany, c. early twentieth century. Cup, 4.25" dia. Saucer, 7.75" dia. $45-75.

*Center left:* Detail of riding scene on Three Crown cup.

Oversize stirrup cup and saucer, VIP series, Royal Worcester, England, c. mid twentieth century. Cup, 4.25" dia. Saucer, 6.5" dia. $95-125.

"Well Cleared" classical hunt motif, Copeland Spode, England, c. mid twentieth century. Cup, 2.75" dia. Saucer, 5.5" dia. $30-50.

Detail of Copeland Spode saucer.

Kaiser coasters in woven wooden basket, Kaiser, W. Germany, c. 1970-present. Coaster, 4" dia. Basket, 7" h. x 5.25" w. $25-45.

Detail of coaster depicting Napoleonic crusade.

Tom and Jerry Punch Bowl set, equestrian design, Universal Cambridge, Made in
U.S.A., c. 1940-50. Bowl, 10.25" dia. Cup, 3" dia. $65-85.

# Chapter 2

# Advertising—Decanters, Labels, Other

"There is no secret so close as that between a rider and his horse."
—Robert Smith Surtees (1803-1864), from "Mr. Sponge's Sporting Tour."

American Thoroughbred liquor decanter, Grenadier Original, c. 1970. 8.75" h. x 7" w. $40-60.

Appaloosa liquor decanter, Grenadier Original, c. 1978. 9" h. x 7" w. $40-60.

Ceramic "Man O' War" on base, manufactured by Heritage China for Ezra Brooks, c. 1969. 11.5" h. $25-45.

Quarter Horse miniature liquor decanter, Hoffman Originals, c. latter twentieth century. Approximately 5.5" h. x 5" w. $25-35.

Shetland Pony miniature liquor decanter, Hoffman Originals, c. latter twentieth century. Approximately 5" h. x 5" w. $25-35.

Arabian Stallion miniature liquor decanter, Hoffman Originals, c. latter twentieth century. Approximately 5.5" h. x 5" w. $25-35.

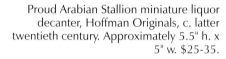

Appaloosa Yearling miniature liquor decanter, Hoffman Originals, c. latter twentieth century. Approximately 5.5" h. x 5" w. $25-35.

Proud Arabian Stallion miniature liquor decanter, Hoffman Originals, c. latter twentieth century. Approximately 5.5" h. x 5" w. $25-35.

Thoroughbred miniature liquor decanter, Hoffman Originals, c. latter twentieth century. Approximately 5.5" h. x 5" w. $25-35.

The years have been kind to White Horse. They have schooled experts in the art of blending the choicest whiskies to the peak of their flavor goodness. And down the long years the fame of White Horse has spread from storied Edinburgh around the world. That's why *everybody likes White Horse!*

86.6 Proof. Browne-Vintners Company, Inc., New York, Sole Distributors

*EVERYBODY LIKES WHITE HORSE BLENDED SCOTCH WHISKY ESTABLISHED 1746

White Horse Whiskey advertisement, "The Favorite," c. 1946. 13.75" h. x 10.75" w. $15-25.

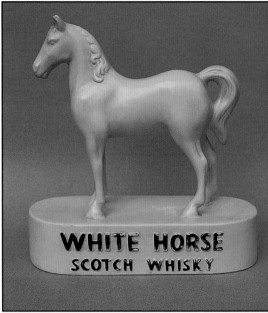

White Horse advertising piece, plaster composition, Made in England, Kelsboro, c. early to mid twentieth century. 9.5" h. x 8" w. $50-70.

Metal advertising piece for Rockmount Ranchwear, c. 1950-60. 6" h. x 5.25" w. $25-35.

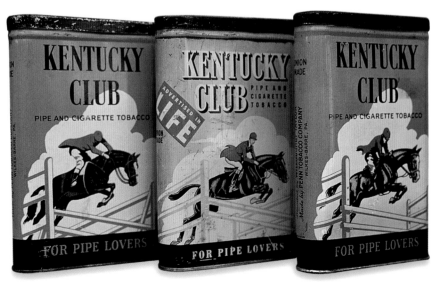

Kentucky Club vertical pocket tobacco tins, manufactured by Penn Tobacco Company, subsequently known as Block Tobacco Company, c. 1930-40. 4.5" h. x 3" w. $15-30 each.

Harvester cigar labels, "Record Breaker" and "Perfecto," horse heads with embossed title and coins, c. 1920-30. 5" h. x 7.5" w. $15-20 each.

Colorful, embossed cut out Trazegnies label, French, c. early twentieth century. 3" h. x 4" w. $15-25.

Colorful, embossed circular Trazegnies label, French, c. early twentieth century. 6" h. x 9" w. $25-35.

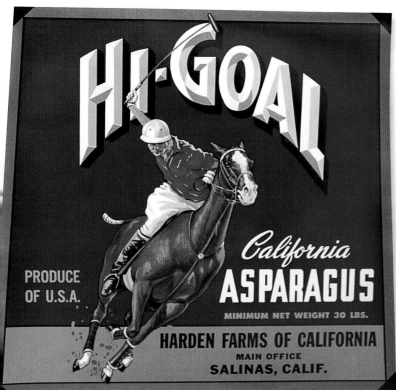

Salinas Asparagus label, Hi-Goal Polo Player, Harden Farms of California, c. 1950. 10" h. x 9.5" w. $20-30.

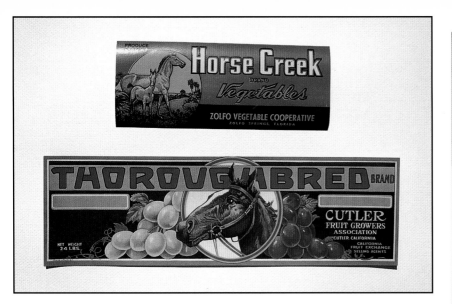

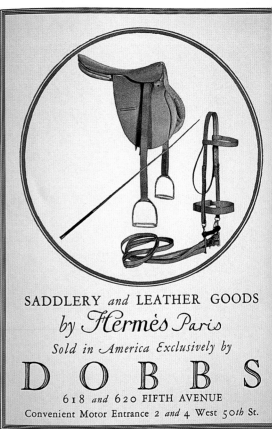

Zolfo Springs Vegetable label, Horse Creek Brand, Zolfo Vegetable Cooperative, c. 1950. 8" h. x 3.75" w. $10-15.

Cutler Grape label, Thoroughbred Brand, Cutler Fruit Growers Association, c. 1920-30. 4" h. x 13.25" w. $20-30.

Dobbs advertisement for Hermes Saddlery and Leather Goods, c. 1920. 9" h. x 7" w. $10-15.

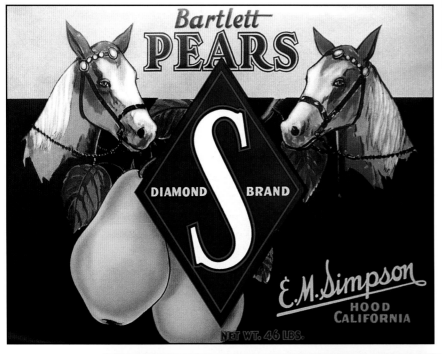

Hood Pear label, Diamond S Brand, E.M. Simpson, c. 1930. 8" h. x 11" w. $20-30.

Saratoga Brand Melon label, San Jose, California, c. 1940-50. 5.25" h. x 13" w. $15-20.

Mustang Brand
Vegetable label,
Guadalupe, California,
c. 1950. 10" h. x 7" w.
$15-25.

Del Monte Vegetable
label, cowboy on
horse watching over
herd, c. 1970.
29.75" h. x 20" w.
$25-45.

Framed cowgirl on palomino with thermometer,
Rome Bakery, East Providence, Rhode Island, c.
1950. 5" h. x 4" w. $25-35.

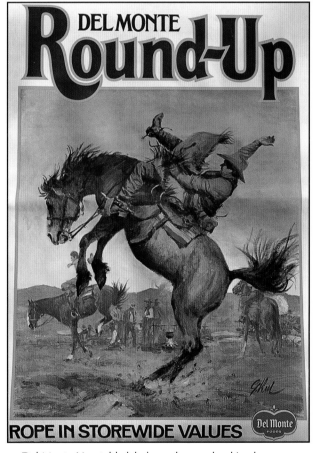

Del Monte Vegetable label, cowboy on bucking bronco,
c. 1970. 29.75" h. x 20" w. $25-45.

## Chapter 3
# Metal

## Bookends

Exquisite two tone horse head bookends, modeled after the Arabian, "Ralet,"
cast gray metal with bronze finish and polished brass highlights, Dodge Inc.,
Inscription: "Gladys Brown," c. 1946. 6.75" h. x 6" w. $150-250.

Stylized horse head bookends mounted on multi-tier metal base, gray metal, bronze finish, Frankart Inc., c. 1930-40. 7.5" h. x 3.5" w. $150-200.

Poised standing horse with English saddle on onyx base, metal figure brass finish, New Diamond, U.S.A., c. mid twentieth century. 7.7" h. x 9.5" w. $90-130.

Abstract grazing pony, hand cast, brass finish on black metal base, Symbol of a Nation Series, Philadelphia Manufacturing Co., c. mid twentieth century. 6" h. x 6.5" w. $95-145.

Polo player on mount, iron, Littco Manufacturing Co. of Wrightsville, Lancaster County, Pennsylvania, c. 1928. 4.5" h. x 3.5" w. $75-95.

Double horse head "Chariot Horses," gray metal, Frankart Inc., c. 1934. 5.5" h. x 5" w. $140-190.

Running colt, gray metal bronze finish, Dodge U.S.A., c. 1940. 4.5" h. x 5.5" w. $95-135.

Attentive mare watching over foal, cast gray metal bronze coating, Dodge Inc., Inscription: "Gladys Brown," c. 1947. 5.5" h. x 7" w. $140-195 for pair.

Hand cast silver colt on black metal base, M.V. Bird and Co., Boston, Massachusetts, c. first half twentieth century. 4.5" h. x 3.75" w. $125-165.

Rearing deco horse, gray metal, Frankart Inc., c. 1934. 5.5" h. x 3.25" w. $110-150.

Adorable foal on base, smooth, rounded lines, Littco Manufacturing Co., c. 1926. 6" h. x 4.5" w. $110-130.

Striking, stylized horse head on base, white metal, bronze finish with copper accent, Trophy Craft Co., Los Angeles, California, c. early twentieth century. $125-175.

Profile of stylized deco horse head on ribbed base, gray metal, bronze finish, highlighted with copper, Champion Products, c. 1935. 8.5" h. x 3.75" w. $150-250.

Artistic, sculpted horse head with geometric flowing lines on tiered base, cast gray metal, bronze finish, copper detailing, Dodge Inc., c. 1936. 7.25" h. x 3.25" w. $135-175.

Iron polo player on metal base, wonderful patina, Littco Manufacturing Co., c. 1928. 5.25" h. x 4.25" w. $90-125.

Intricately detailed horse head bookend, cast gray metal, bronze finish, brass wash, Dodge Inc., Inscription: "Gladys Brown," c. 1946. 6.25" h. x 6" w. $150-250 for pair.

Hand cast standing silver metal horse on ornately sculptured base, bookend/ashtray, Philadelphia Manufacturing Co., c. 1940-60. 6" h. x 5.5" w. $125-175.

Alert standing foal on detailed metal base, gray metal, finished in bronze, copper highlights, Champion Products, Inscription: "PHILLIPE DI NAPOLI" (artist), c. 1930. 7.25" h. x 6" w. $150-250.

Distinctively styled art deco horse head bookends, cast white metal, bronze with copper detailing, signed, c. 1920-30. 7.25" h. x 4.25" w. $120-150.

Percheron bookends, Virginia Metal Crafters, c. 1950. 5.5" h. x 6.5" w. $80-95.

Empty saddle bookends, copper plated iron, unmarked, c. 1930. 4.75" h. x 5.25" w. $50-70.

"End of the Trail" bookends, modeled after a statue by James Earle Frazer, b. 1876, polychrome, Ronson, c. 1925. 6" h. x 4.5" w. $120-145.

"End of the Trail" iron, Littco Manufacturing Co., c. 1926. 6" h. x 5.5" w. $90-130.

# Figures and Associated Metal Pieces

Detail of ornate and highly detailed metal horse figure, bridle and breast plate inset with red stones, Estes Tarter (artist), c. mid twentieth century. 16.5" h. x 14" w. $200-275.

Vintage western copper lamp featuring horse on base with copper shade, unmarked, c. 1940-1950. 11" h. $75-95.

Detail of silver horse statue.

Elegant silver standing horse on base, outfitted in western tack, removable saddle, Estes Tarter (artist), c. mid twentieth century. 8.5" h. x 8" w. $100-150.

Statue of cowboy riding bucking bronco, white metal with copper finish, unmarked, c. 1940-50. 5.5" h. x 4.5" w. $25-45.

Carnival western horse, metal, copper finish, unmarked, c. 1940-50. 8.75" h. x 12" w. $45-60.

Painted metal souvenir horses, Japan, c. 1950-60. Small horse, 3.25" h. x 3.75" w. $25-35. Large horse, 4.5" h. x 5.5" w. $40-55.

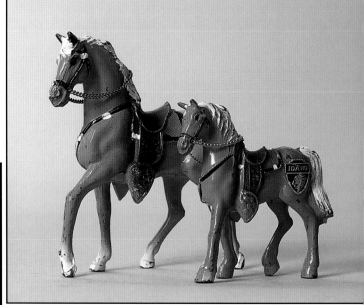

Empty saddle doorstop, unmarked, c. mid twentieth century. 8.75" h. x 10" w. $125-175.

Metal horse with copper finish mounted on base with ashtray and two pipe holders, unmarked, c. 1940-50. 5.5" h. x 7.5" w. $40-65.

Fount-O-Ink horse inkwell, bronze with copper wash and beautiful patina, c. 1912-13. 3.75" h. x 8.75" w. $120-145.

Souvenir copper salt and pepper shakers, front features horse head marked "Butte," reverse is horse's hoof, c. 1950-60. 2" h. x 2.75" w. $25-40.

Rearing horse table lighter, chrome, MTC, Japan, c. 1940-50. 5" h. x 3.5" w. $45-65.

"Man O' War" tile framed in copper, unmarked, c. 1930-50. 5.25" h. x 5.25" w. $40-65.

Detail of Hubley horse on ashtray.

Brown Hubley horse on horseshoe ashtray, Hubley Manufacturing Co., Lancaster, Pennsylvania, c. 1930. 3.5" h. x 4" w. $75-100.

Brass ashtray with horse head emblem in center and rests on ends, decorative border, Mitchell, Canada, c. 1940-60. 3.75" h. x 7.5" w. $35-55.

Bronze prancing horse on oval ashtray base, K. & O. Co., Made in U.S.A., c. 1920-40. 4" h. x 3.5" w. $60-80.

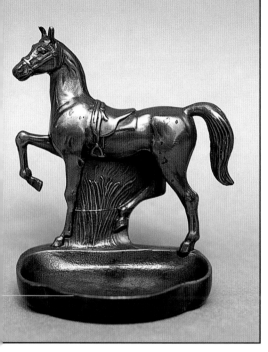

Bronze high stepping horse with English saddle on valet base, K. & O. Co. Made in U.S.A., c. 1920-40. 4" h. x 3.5" w. $55-75.

Metal jockey on horse combination ashtray and pipe holders, copper wash, Philadelphia Manufacturing Co., c. 1940. 4.75" h. x 8.25" w. $50-70.

Bronze figural horse on raised base, flanked by pipe holder on each side, K. & O. Co., Made in U.S.A., c. 1948. 5.25" h. x 6.5" w. $65-85.

Comical bronze horse ashtray, K. & O. Co., Made in U.S.A., c. 1920-40. 3.5" h. x 6.5" w. $60-80.

Whimsical pony pipe holder, solid bronze, unmarked, c. 1920-40. 4" h. x 4" w. $70-90.

Caricature bronze pony, K. & O. Co., Made in U.S.A., c. 1920-40. 4.5" h. x 4" w. $50-70.

Flirtatious solid bronze colt, K. & O. Co., Made in U.S.A., c. 1920-40. 4.25" h. x 4.25" w. $80-120.

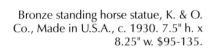

Bronze standing horse statue, K. & O. Co., Made in U.S.A., c. 1930. 7.5" h. x 8.25" w. $95-135.

Victorian style cast metal horse statue, clock ornament, unmarked, c. late nineteenth/early twentieth century. 7.75" h. x 8.5" w. $60-90.

Hand cast playful trio of bronze colts, unmarked, c. early twentieth century. 6.75" h. x 10" w. $250+.

Sleek, elegant bronze deco style sculpture, highlighted with brass, unmarked, c. twentieth century. 8" h. x 13" w. $400+.

Prancing horse on rectangular base, white metal, air brushed, unmarked, c. 1944. 10" h. x 9.5" w. $75-95.

Uniquely styled painted horse head with two brass cup inserts, unmarked, c. 1920. 6" h. x 8" w. $200+.

Brass horse head bottle opener/corkscrew combination, Inscription: "Chicago," c. 1940-50. 2" h. x 4.25" w. $30-45.

Standing brass horse on bronze base with thermometer, Churchill Downs, Louisville, Kentucky, c. early twentieth century. 4.5" h. x 4.75" w. $65-95.

Bronze horse mounted on ivory metal base with thermometer. Thermometer made by Rochester Manufacturing Co. Inc., Rochester, New York, c. early twentieth century. 3.75" h. x 5.25" w. $55-75.

Rearing metal horse bank on pebbled base, unmarked, possibly Arcade, c. 1910, or A.C. Williams, c. 1910-34. 7.5" h. x 6.5" w. $95-125.

Black iron horse bank, "My Pet," Arcade, c. 1920. 4.25" h. x 5.25" w. $150-175.

Iron horse head paperweight, unmarked, c. 1930. 5" h. x 4" w. $75-95.

Iron horse head hitching post topper, unmarked, c. 1900-20. 10" h. x 7.75" w. $300+.

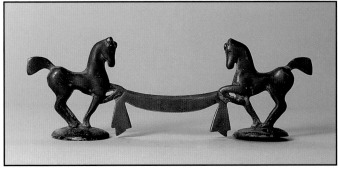

Brass horse boot scraper, deco style horses, Virginia Metal Crafters, Waynesboro, Virginia, c. 1920. 4" h. x 12" w. $150-225.

Cinderella carriage doorstop, original paint, Spanora, c. 1920-30. 7.25" h. x 16.75" w. $250+.

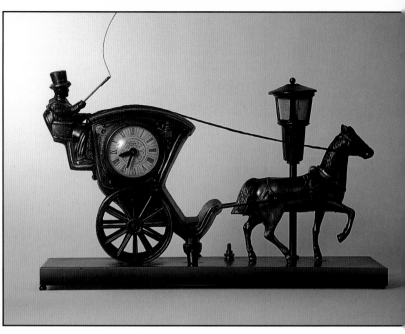

Mantel clock with horse drawn buggy, animated whip, and illuminated light, bronze finish, United Metal Goods Manufacturing Co. Inc., Brooklyn, New York, c. early twentieth century. 10" h. x 16" w. $195-250.

Silver art deco horse clock, Howard Clock Co., c. 1940. 9.75" h. x 9" w. $95-125.

Souvenir horse and clock on wood base, brass finish, United Clock Co., c. 1940-50. 11.5" h. x 16.25" w. $125-175.

Horse drawn coach on metal base, copper finish, United Clock Co.,
c. 1933. 7.5" h. x 17.25" w. $175-250.

Ornate Cinderella coach drawn by horse with riders, brass on wood base, United
Clock Co., c. 1940-50. 9" h. x 21.5" w. $125-175.

# Chapter 4
# *Apparel and Textiles*

Lovely 1917 calendar on brown cardstock with printed grid and ribboned layers. Lady with riding crop over shoulders, unmarked, c. 1917. 8.5" h. x 4.5" w. $45-65.

"We shall take care not to vex the young horse or cause it to abandon its affable gracefulness in disgust. For this is like the fragrance of blossoms, which never returns, once it has vanished."

—Antoine de la Baume Pluvinel (c. 1600)

## *Apparel*

*For Madame and Mademoiselle*

### RIDING HABITS

*Conservative — Conventional — Correct*

### READY FOR IMMEDIATE WEARING

Smart Accessories too.

THE RIDING HABIT SHOP—*Fifth Floor*

## Franklin Simon & Co.

*A Store of Individual Shops*

Fifth Avenue, 37th and 38th Streets, New York

Entire contents copyrighted, 1925, by FRANKLIN SIMON & CO., INC.

Advertisement for riding habits featured at Franklin Simon & Co., New York, c. 1925. 9" h. x 7" w. $10-20.

Gentlemen's English riding apparel advertisement, Bernard Weatherill, New York, c. 1925. 9" h. x 7" w. $10-20.

Colorful ad for the Alfred Nelson Co., tailors and practical breeches makers, New York, c. 1925. 9" h. x 7" w. $10-20.

"The Fortmasson Saunterer," hat advertisement, Best & Co., New York, c. 1925. 9" h. x 7" w. $10-20.

English riding hat with chin strap, blu[ ] mesh, and satin flowers, c. 1930-4[ ] 11" dia. $45-65.

Lady's wool top hat with chin strap, Tally Ho, England, c. early twentieth century. 10.5" dia. $95-125.

# Needlepoint, Fabric, Tapestry

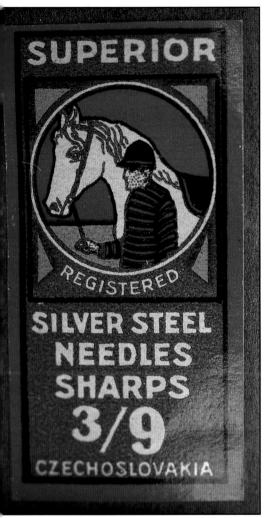

European sewing card, Czechoslovakia, c. 1920. 4.75" h. x 4.5" w. $30-45.

Package of Superior silver steel needles, Czechoslovakia, c. 1920. 2" h. x 1" w. $5-10.

Framed gray horse head needlepoint, wool on canvas, c. early to mid twentieth century. 15.75" h. x 13" w. $50-75.

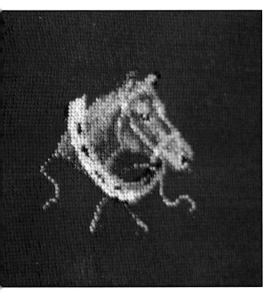

Petit-point horse head encircled by horseshoe, wool on canvas, c. early twentieth century. 7.75" h. x 7.5" w. $65-85.

*Top left:* Traditional hunt scene combination needlepoint and petit-point pillow, c. mid twentieth century. 10" h. x 10" w. $40-65.

*Top right:* Motif of lady riding side saddle delicately embroidered on linen, c. 1920-40. 20" h. x 14" w. $10-20.

*Center:* Vintage quilted pillow with grazing horse design, c. 1950. 10" h. x 19" w. $35-45.

*Bottom right:* Gray horse head appliqué doily, hand stitched on linen with scalloped edge, c. 1930. 8" h. x 5" w. $10-15.

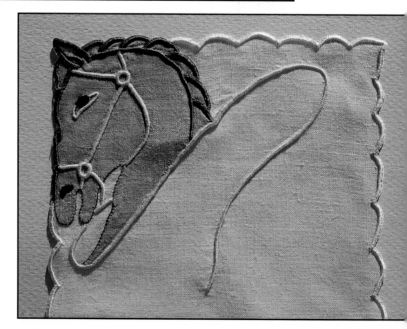

Embroidered horse head placemat, hand stitched on linen with green edging, c. 1940-50. 13.5" h. x 19.5" w. $20-30.

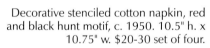

Cotton pillowcase, hand embroidered with scene of horses and flowers, c. 1950. 29" h. x 21" w. $30-45 per set.

Decorative stenciled cotton napkin, red and black hunt motif, c. 1950. 10.5" h. x 10.75" w. $20-30 set of four.

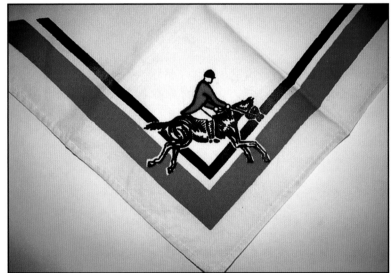

Steeplechase scene stenciled in color on cotton tablecloth, c. 1950. 33.25" h. x 31.5" w. $25-40.

Polished cotton fabric panel depicting hunters at rest in muted tones of lilac, apricot, gold, and green, c. 1920-30. $10-15 per panel.

Beautiful vintage silk horse scarf, brown horse head design on ivory background, c. 1940-50. 30" h. x 30" w. $30-50.

Western cowboy fabric panels, Quadriga drip-dry cloth, E & W Brand, c. 1950. $10-20 per yard.

Woven French tapestry with theme of riding to the hounds, Made in France, c. twentieth century. 25" h. x 48" w. $75-125.

Detail of French tapestry, lady riding sidesaddle over fence.

Detail of French tapestry, rider sounding horn to hounds

Elegant French tapestry picturing hunters on horseback with pack in pursuit of game, Made in France, c. twentieth century. 50" h. x 64" w. $175-250.

*Chapter 5*
# Wood

"We have almost forgotten how strange a thing it is that so huge and powerful and intelligent an animal as a horse should allow another, and far more feeble animal, to ride upon its back."
—Peter Gray (b. 1928)

## Bookends

Arabian horse head bookends, wood composite,
unmarked, c. 1940, 6.25" h. x 5" w. $35-65.

Horse head relief on wooden stand, combination wood composite and wood, Syrocowood, Syracuse, New York, c. 1940. 6.5" h. x 5.5" w. $40-70.

Another view of raised horse head mounted on wood.

Detailed horse head with bridle bookends, unmarked, c. 1940-50. 6.5" h. x 6" w. $40-60.

Mare and foal bookends on metal base, Syrocowood, New York, c. 1930. 6.25" h. x 5.25" w. $40-70.

Horse and setter bookends with metal base, Syrocowood, New York, c. 1930. 7" h. x 5.25" w. $40-70.

Triple horse head bookend, wood composite, unmarked, c. 1940. 6.75" h. x 7" w. $40-70.

Nicely detailed, raised horse head surrounded by horseshoe, Syrocowood, Syracuse, New York, c. 1930. 6.5" h. x 5" w. $40-70.

Bookends showing hunters riding horses through the woods, Syrocowood, Syracuse, New York, c. 1930. 7" h. x 5" w. $40-75.

Bookends featuring single bridled horse head set over crossed riding crops, Syrocowood, Syracuse, New York, c. 1930-40. 6.25" h. x 4.5" w. $45-70.

Single horse head brush holder, Syrocowood, New York, c. 1930. 7" h. x 5.75" w. $25-40.

Brush holder featuring single bridled horse head set over crossed riding crops, Syrocowood, Syracuse, New York, c. 1930-40. 6" h. x 4.5" w. $30-45.

Horse head double brush holder, Ornawood, U.S.A., c. 1930-40. 5.5" h. x 8" w. $25-40.

Standing horse brush holder accented with color, manufactured by Burwood Products Inc., Travers City, c. 1930-40. 5.5" h. x 6" w. $30-45.

Horse head bottle openers, Syrocowood, New York, c. 1930. 4.25" h. x 5" w. $20-30 each.

Tie and belt holder, single bridled horse head with English motif, Syrocowood, Syracuse, New York, c. 1930-50. 7" h. x 12.75" w. $35-60.

Tie and belt holder with raised horse head and English detailing, Syrocowood, Syracuse, New York, c. 1930-50. 7" h. x 13" w. $40-65.

Detail of horse head relief on tie and belt holder.

Decorative horse head perpetual calendar, Ornawood, U.S.A., c. 1940. 3.5" h. x 7" w. $35-65.

Horse head thermometer, wood composite, unmarked, thermometer made in U.S.A., c. 1940. 4" h. x 3.5" w. $25-35.

Carved wooden horse with glass eyes on fancy base, unmarked, c. 1950. 4.75" h. x 5.5" w. $40-60.

Comical, smiling bony horse on base, wood composite, unmarked, c. 1930. 4.5" h. x 5" w. $20-30.

Multiple pipe holder with horse and dogs, horse has glass eyes, Syrocowood, U.S.A., c. 1930. 6.75" h. x 9.25" w. $30-50.

Wooden pipe rack with double horse head topper, seven slots, unmarked, c. 1930-50. 7.75" h. x 11" w. $35-50. Shown with carved horse head pipe with glass eyes, handcrafted, Made in Italy, c. mid twentieth century. 2.75" h. x 6" w. $40-60.

Set of wooden coasters with stand, horse head appliqué on coasters, unmarked, c. 1950-60. Coaster, 3.5" dia. Base, 4" dia. $25-35.

Top view of coasters above.

# Chapter 6

# Literature—Books, Pamphlets, Magazines

"A horse can lend the speed and strength he or she lacks—but the rider who is wise remembers it is no more than a loan."
—Pam Brown (b. 1928)

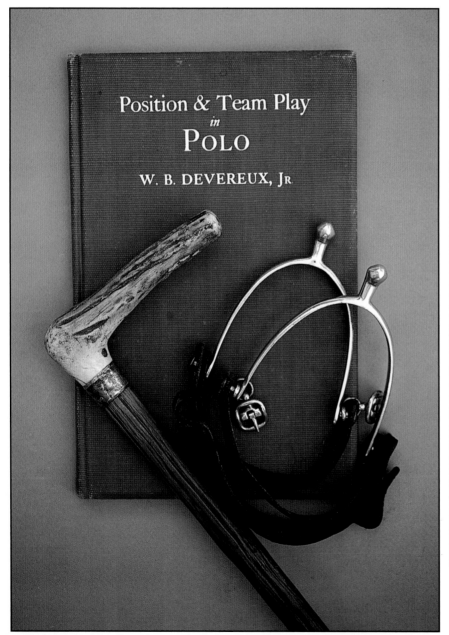

Book, *Position & Team Play in Polo*, by W.B. Devereux, Jr., Mineola, New York, The Davenport Press Inc., 1924. Blue cloth binding. 9.5" h. x 6.25" w. $30-50. Shown with English spurs and bone handled riding crop.

»» Inferno ««

Winner of The King's Plate, 1905

Color plate of "Inferno," winner of the Kings Plate, 1905, from *The Queens Plate*, by Trent Frayne, Canada, The Hunter Rose Co. Ltd., 1959. 10.25" h. x 7" w. $25-40.

Book, *The Maryland Hunt Club*, by Stuart Rose, first edition, New York, Huntington Press, 1931. Green cloth binding with embossed seal of hunter over fence, title page. 11" h. x 7.75" w. $60-85.

# THE MARYLAND HUNT CUP

### By STUART ROSE

*With a Foreword by Jacob A. Ulman and a Chart of the Course by Gordon Ross*

## HUNTINGTON PRESS

*New York : 1931*

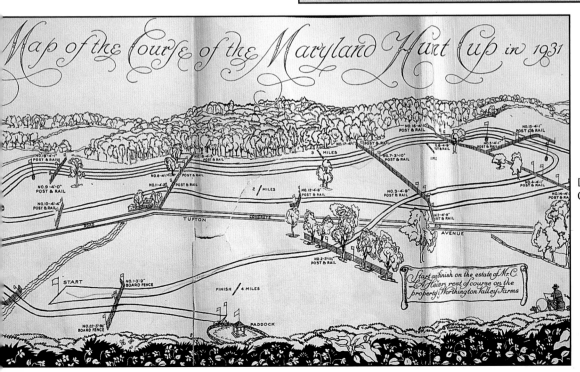

Detail of Maryland Hunt Club Course, 1931.

Book, *Official Horse Shows Blue Book*, New York, J.W. Waring Publishing Co., Volume 38, 1944. Semi-soft cover with gold gilded title. 9" h. x 6.75" w. $80-120.

Detail of Mrs. P.A. Thomas, Jr. with "Big Shot," from *Official Horse Shows Blue Book*, 1944.

Detail of "Cornish Hills" from *Official Horse Shows Blue Book*, 1944.

Detail of "Clearview Maybelle" from *Official Horse Shows Blue Book*, 1944.

Book, *Currier & Ives* by Harry T. Peters, Garden City, New York, Doubleday Doran Publishers, 1942. This special edition is set in twelve point caslon monotype with hand-drawn decorative initials. Front cover features print, "The Road-Winter," portraying Nathaniel Currier and his wife. 12.5" h. x 9.25" w. $50-70.

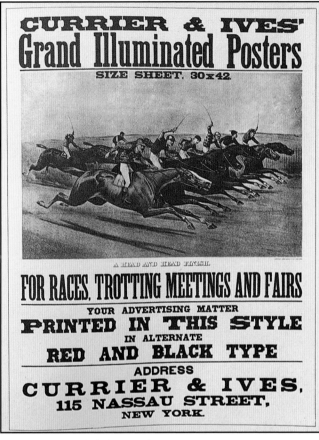

Detail of Plate 85, from *Currier & Ives*, 1942.

Detail of Plate 79, "Trotting Cracks" at the Forge, from *Currier & Ives*, 1942.

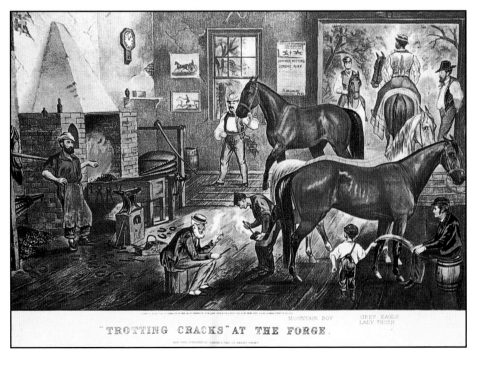

Book, *Nimrod's Hunting Tours, Interspersed with Characteristic Anecdotes, Sayings and Doings of Sporting Men*, by C.J. Apperley, first edition, London, M.A. Pittman, 1835. Marbled boards, gilt edged pages. 8.75" h. x 5.5" w. $200+.

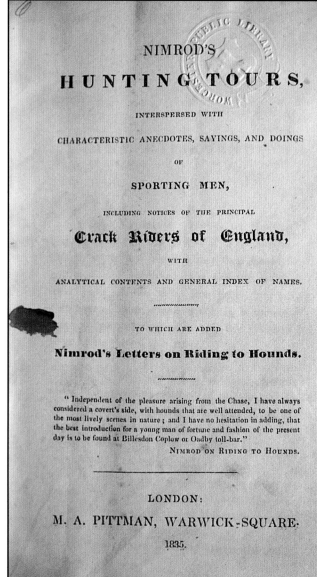

Detail of title page from *Nimrod's Hunting Tours*, 1835.

Book, *Biggle Horse Book*, by Jacob Biggle, Philadelphia, Wilmer Atkinson Company, 1913. Practical and concise information on the horse. 5.5" h. x 3.75" w. $40-60.

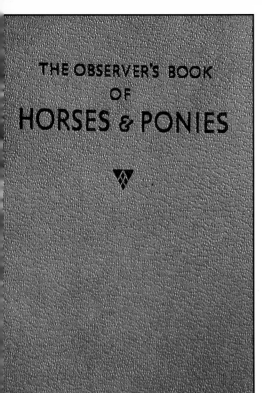

Book, *The Observer's Book of Horses & Ponies*, by R.S. Summerhays, London, England, Frederick Warne & Co. Ltd., 1961. Illustrations and descriptions for over one hundred breeds and varieties of horses and ponies. 5.75" h. x 3.75" w. $15-25.

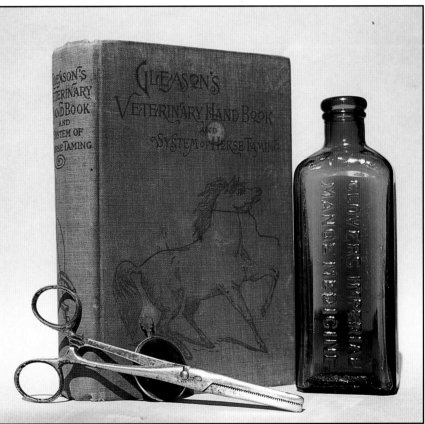

Detail of frontispiece from *The Observer's Book of Horses & Ponies*, 1961.

Book, *Gleason's Horse Book*, by Professor Oscar R. Gleason, Springfield, Ohio, The Crowell & Kirkpatrick Co., 1892. Softcover book by America's King of Horse Trainers. 7.5" h. x 5.25" w. $75-100.

Book, *Gleason's Veterinary Hand Book and System of Horse Taming*, by Oliver W. Gleason, Chicago, Charles C. Thompson Co., 1914. A two part book dedicated to veterinary science and horse taming. 8" h. x 5.5" w. $80-120. Shown with veterinary tools and glass bottle marked Clovers Imperial Mange Medicine.

Book, *The Horse and Its Illnesses*, by B.J. Kendall, M.D., Cleveland, Ohio, Lauer and Yost, Publisher, 1880. 7.5" h. x 4.75" w. $40-60.

Pamphlet, *Nutrition of Horses*, Canada, published by Master Feeds, October, 1968. 9" h. x 6" w. $8-12.

## JUSTIN MORGAN
### The Founder of a Great Breed

WHETHER Justin Morgan was the son of True Briton (known also as Beautiful Bay) and out of a daughter of Diamond, get of Church's Wildair, nothing pertaining to his origin could possibly be said that would add to or detract from his place in equine history. Justin Morgan stands unrivalled—the *fountain-head* of the first great family of American horses.

That Justin Morgan was rich in the blood of Thoroughbreds and Arabians, through both his sire and dam is certain. In any event, there converged in this single animal an inheritance of not only extraordinary individual excellence but a prepotency which carried this excellence through generation after generation.

This distinguished animal, foaled in 1789, got the name-by which he has been known for over a hundred years from the man who bred him and was his owner until late in 1795. The man, Justin Morgan, was born in 1747 at West Springfield, Massachusetts, where he lived until 1788, when he moved to Randolph, Vermont. He died in the latter place in March 1798.

While owned by Justin Morgan, the horse was known as "Figure" and probably made his first season in the stud at West Hartford, Connecticut in 1792. In the years 1793, 4 and 5, Mr. Morgan advertised him as standing in Randolph and nearby Vermont towns. Subsequently he had a succession of owners, but the sum of his career in the stud was the establishment of a type that endures after a century and a half of frequent change in demand and emphasis.

Justin Morgan was a dark bay with black legs, mane and tail. His high head was sharply cut; his dark eyes were prominent, lively and pleasant; his wide-set ears were small, pointed and erect; his round body was short-backed, close-ribbed and deep; his thin legs were set wide and straight, and the pasterns and shoulders were sloping; his action was straight, bold and vigorous; his style was proud, nervous and imposing. In a word, Justin Morgan was a beautifully symmetrical, stylish, vibrant animal, renowned for looks, manners and substance. He died from an injury at the age of 32—in 1821.

- 1 -

Detail of "Justin Morgan, Founder of a Great Breed" taken from soft cover pamphlet, *The Morgan Horse*, New York, The Morgan Horse Club, 1937. 9.25" h. x 6.25" w. $10-15.

## The Morgan Is Famed For Its Great Endurance

FROM Justin Morgan down, the Morgan horse has been noted for his stamina. D. C. Linsley, in his book, "Morgan Horses," published in 1857, quoted a letter from Solomon Steel, dated Derby Line, Vermont, March 12, 1856, in which the writer said, "It has been my privilege, in early life, to often see the original Morgan horse, called by this name from the fact that Justin Morgan brought him to Randolph, Vermont, from Massachusetts in the Autumn of 1795." Referring to the horse's individual excellence, Mr. Steel wrote, "he was then found able to out-draw, out-walk, out-trot, or out-run every horse that was matched against him, * * * he could not be beaten where strength, speed and endurance were the test."

The endurance so characteristic of the Morgan was unquestionably one of the important factors which led to the quick distribution of Morgan blood throughout the country. In the list of fourteen sires selected as foundation stock by the National Saddle-Horse Breeders' Association, organized in Kentucky, in 1891, four of the stallions were *registered* Morgans.

J. H. Sanders, founder of *The Breeder's Gazette*, wrote in 1891: "The investigation into the pedigrees of the trotting horses of America, in preparation of the Breeder's Trotting Stud Book, has led us to put a higher estimate upon the blood of Black Hawk (sired by Sherman Morgan, in turn by Justin Morgan) than has generally been accorded to him by writers upon the trotting horse. Indeed, * * * we are inclined to the opinion that the name of but one horse, Rysdyk's Hambletonian, will be found more frequently in the pedigrees of standard-bred trotters." And be it remembered that the greatest son of Hambletonian (George Wilkers) was out of a mare (Dolly Spanker) having Morgan blood.

300-Mile Endurance Rides fostered by various horse associations, the U. S. Department of Agriculture and the U. S. Remount Service, were held annually from 1920 to 1927. The distance was sixty miles a day for five consecutive days, the weight carried from 200 to 245 pounds, and the time for each sixty miles from nine to ten hours. The great distance travelled, the heavy weight carried, and the limited time used, speak for the

record of the pure-bred Morgans in these rides gave further proof of their exceptional sturdiness.

More recently the Green Mountain Horse Association has sponsored annual 100-Mile contests over the rugged Vermont country roads and mountain trails. Morgans have won these contests in 1937, 1939 and 1941, over large fields of contestants including representatives of the other light breeds of horses. The Morgan horse's stamina and reliability, account for its great popularity on the trails in both the Eastern and Western country, and for its superiority as a stock horse

*Upwey Princess, by Upwey Prince Tarik 7861 and out of a mare containing some Morgan blood. Winner of the 1939 One Hundred Mile Trail Ride of Green Mountain Horse Association.*

*Sudwin 0-4746, by John A. Darling 7470 and out of Gladwin 0876 by Ethan Allen 3rd. Winner of both the Vermont and Maine One Hundred Mile Trail Rides in 1941.*

*Gladstone 4822, bus 1915, by General Gates. Won second out of a field of 21 starters in the 1927 Eastern Endurance Ride, with the same score on "condition" as received by the winner.*

Excerpt from *The Morgan Horse*.

Pamphlets and magazine, *How to Ride and Train the Western Horse*, by Pete Moss, c. 1967. $10-15; *Western Story Magazine*, various authors, March, 1938. $10-20; *Western Horseman*, Quarter Horse Special, various authors, June, 1954. $10-15. Also shown is a sculpted metal show saddle.

Pamphlet, *Professor Beery's Saddle Horse Instructions*, by Beery School of Horsemanship, Pleasant Hill, Ohio, 1963. Soft cover, book five of series. 8.5" h. x 5.25" w. $10-15.

Magazine cover, *Country Gentleman*, July, 1926. Cover illustration by N.C. Wyeth. 14" h. x 11" w. $20-30.

Magazine cover, *The Spur,* September, 1936. Cover illustration from the painting, "Little Silver," by Carl Kahler. 14" h. x 10" w. $20-30.

Magazine cover, *The Spur,* May, 1, 1932. Cover illustration from the painting, "In Central Park," by Harry S. Lane. 14.5" h. x 10" w. $20-30.

Book, *Portfolio of Horse Paintings,* by Wesley Dennis. Chicago, New York, San Francisco, Rand McNally & Company, 1964. Commentary by Marguerite Henry. 15" h. x 12.5" w. $25-40.

Illustration from *Portfolio of Horse Paintings,* "The Arab" by Wesley Dennis.

Illustration from *Portfolio of Horse Paintings,* "The Lipizzan" by Wesley Dennis.

Book, *The Spanish Riding School in Vienna,* by Ann Tizia Leitich, München, Germany, Nymphenburger Verlagshandlung GmbH, 1956. Preface by Colonel A. Podhajsky. 8" h. x 7" w. $30-45.

Detail from *The Spanish Riding School in Vienna*. Horse and rider demonstrating the Courbette, one of the most difficult jumps of haute école.

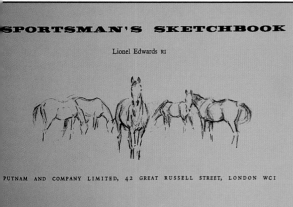

Book, *Sportsman's Sketchbook,* by Lionel Edwards RI, London, England, Putnam and Company Limited, not dated. 5.5" h. x 8.25" w. $65-85.

Illustration from *Sportsman's Sketchbook* by Lionel Edwards RI, "The Jumping Lane."

Illustration from *Sportsman's Sketchbook* by Lionel Edwards RI, "Hunting Morn."

## Chapter 7
# *Glass*

### *Bookends*

Red glass rearing horse bookends,
L.E. Smith, c. 1940-50. 8" h. x
5" w. $125-150.

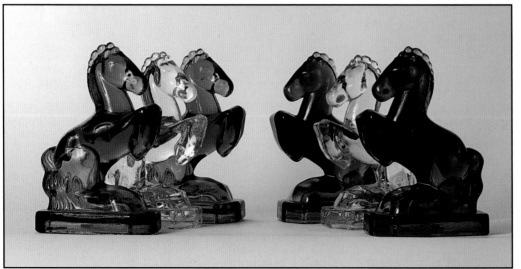

Amber, clear, and green rearing
horse bookends, L.E. Smith, c.
1940-50. 8" h. x 5" w. Clear glass,
$80-100. Colored glass, $125-150
per pair.

Clear glass rearing horse bookends, New Martinsville Glass Company, c. 1940. 7.5" h. x 6" w. $140-165.

Frosted glass rearing horse bookends, New Martinsville Glass Company, c. 1940. 7.5" h. x 6" w. $150-175.

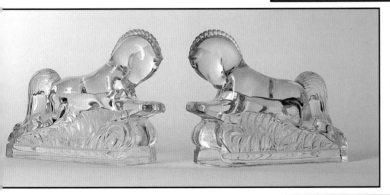

Clear glass jumping horse, bookends, unmarked, c. 1940. 7.25" h. x 10" w. $100-125.

Clear glass horse head bookends, Federal Glass, c. 1940. 5.5" h. x 5.5" w. $15-35.

Blue glass horse vase, L.E. Smith,
c. 1960-70. 5" h. x 4.75" w. $45-65.

Exquisite crystal horse head on base, Serres,
France, c. latter twentieth century. 3.5" h. x
5" w. $135-155.

"Little Joe" the horse in
burnt orange and sea
foam green, Boyd,
c. latter twentieth
century. 4" h. x 3.75" w.
$20-30 each.

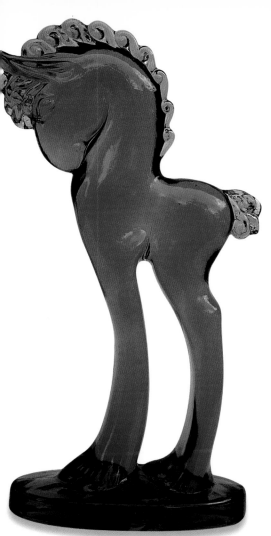

Emerald green glass pony, Mosser, c. mid to latter twentieth century. 5.5" h. x 3.5" w. $20-35.

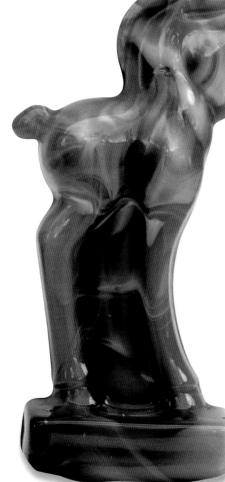

Caramel slag glass standing colt, Heisey/Imperial, c. 1969-77. 5" h. x 2" w. $30-45.

Glass pony trio, emerald and oblique custard ponies manufactured by Mosser, caramel slag pony by Heisey/Imperial.

Souvenir glass ashtray with plastic standing horse, c. 1940. 3.25" h. x 3" w. $20-25.

Depression era glass dish with deco pony center, made from eight part press, c. 1920-30. 3.5" h. x 5.5" w. $30-45.

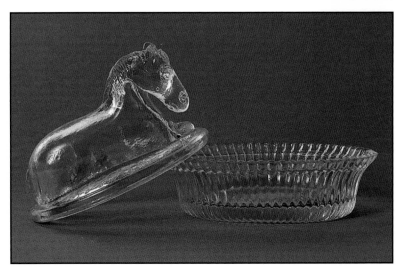

Clear glass covered dish with resting horse as cover, c. mid twentieth century. 4.25" h. x 5.75" w. $20-30.

White glass cup with two deco style horse head handles, gives off luminescent glow indicating uranium content, unmarked, c. 1930. 3.75" h. x 5.5" w. $25-35.

Milk glass coasters with brass rim, "Seabiscuit," Lynn Bogue Hunt, (artist), "High Gun," Sintzenich, (artist), manufactured by Trayette, c. early-mid twentieth century. 4.5" dia. $35-55 each.

Milk glass coaster with sterling silver rim, "Man O War," Lynn Bogue Hunt, (artist), manufactured by Graf, Washington & Dunn, c. 1899-1961. 4.5" dia. $50-70.

Clear glass with black horse head design, signed, c. 1950. Shot glass, 2.25" h. $3-6. Glass, 5.2" h. $5-8.

Detail of shot glass, black horse head with red bridle.

Vintage equestrian scene shaker and glasses, signed, c. 1950. Glasses, 3" h. $3-5 each. Shaker, 8" h. $10-15.

Hunt scene glassware, unmarked, c. 1950. 5.75" h. $5-8 each.

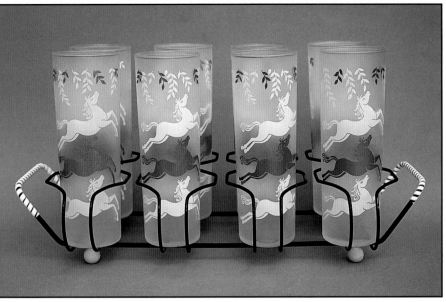

Vintage set of frosted glasses, detailed with white and metallic gold horses in rack, Libby, c. 1950. Glass, 7" h. $45-55 set.

Elegant crystal sherry, bridle rosette pattern, manufactured by Cambridge Glass Co., c. 1908. 4" h. x 2" w. $20-25.

Detail of sherry base exhibiting bridle rosette pattern.

Hand painted horse and rider cordial glasses rimmed in gold, unmarked, c. mid twentieth century. 3.5" h. x 2.5" w. $15-20 each.

Set of multi-colored liquor glasses detailed with gold, unmarked,
c. mid twentieth century. 3.25" h. x 3" w. $25-40.

Detail of blue liquor glass emblazoned
with horse and rider demonstrating
the Capriole.

# Decanters, Other

Muted pink Depression era seven piece cordial set, decorated with ivory tone enamel, France, c. early twentieth century. Glasses, 2" h. x 1.25" w. Decanter, 7.5" h. x 4.25" w. $60-90 set.

Exquisite turquoise frosted glass decanter and cordials with gold overlay depicting equestrian motif, c. mid twentieth century. Glasses, 2.5" h. x 1.5" w. Decanter, 11" h. x 4" w. $75-100 set.

Trojan horse design martini set, pitcher, glasses and glass rod stirrer, by Fred Press, c. 1950. Glasses, 3" h. Pitcher, 10.25" h. $50-75 set.

Colorful fox hunt tray, reverse painted glass, Made in Japan, possibly during Occupied period, c. 1950. 8.75" dia. $35-50.

Rectangular horseracing foil art tray with reverse painted glass, framed in maple, unmarked, c. 1940. 13" h. x 19" w. with 1" handles. $25-40.

Vibrant reverse painting under glass in oval mahogany frames, resembles "Napoleon Crossing the Alps," unmarked, c. 1930-40. 8.75" h. x 6" w. $150-200 pair.

*Chapter 8*

# Jewelry

"A good horse and a good rider are only so in mutual trust."
—H.M.E.

## Pins and Brooches

Brilliant deco Trifari silver horse head pin with black enamel and white rhinestones, c. 1924-present. 2.25" h. x 2" w. $120–150.

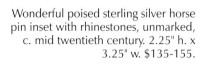

Wonderful poised sterling silver horse pin inset with rhinestones, unmarked, c. mid twentieth century. 2.25" h. x 3.25" w. $135-155.

Swirling, sterling silver seahorse, signed Lang, c. 1946 and beyond. 3.75" h. x 2.5" w. $90-120.

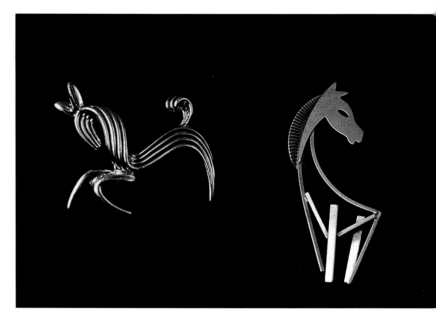

Left: Dancing silver horse pin, Emmons, c. 1949-1980. 2" h. x 1.75" w. $50-75.
Right: Sterling geometric horse pin, Beau, c. 1947-present. 2.5" h. x 1" w. $65-85.

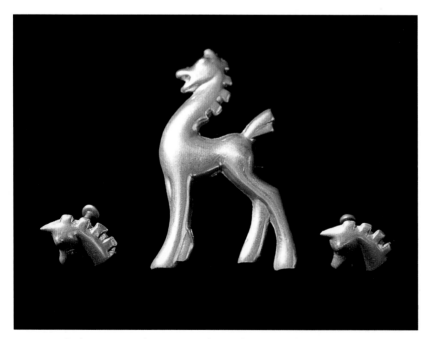

Extremely deco, pewter horse pin with matching screw back earrings, Howard Pierce, c. early to mid twentieth century. Pin, 2.5" h. x 1.25" w. Earrings, .75" h. $275-300.

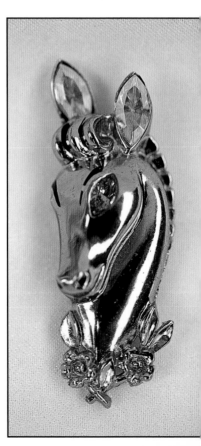

Goldtone horse head fur clip inset with faceted stones, Coro, c. 1919-1979. 2" h. x .75" w. $80-130.

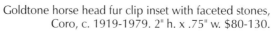

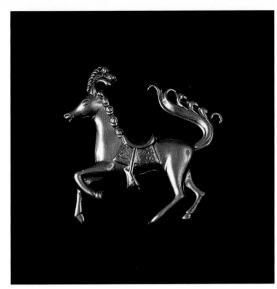

Fancy sterling silver circus horse pin, signed Lang, c. 1946 and beyond. 1.75" h. x 1.75" w. $50-75.

Decorative sterling silver horse pin with pink and blue rhinestones, unmarked, c. 1940. 2.5" h. x 2" w. $50-65.

Delicate Beau sterling mare and colt brooch, c. 1950. .78" h. x 1.5" w. $45-65.

Balking colt pin, marked S.B. Sterling, c. 1950. 2.25" h. x 1.5" w. $45-65.

Brilliant rhinestone horse pin, Trifari, c. 1924-present. .75" h. x 1" w. $60-90.

Intricate silver repoussé horse head brooch, unmarked, c. early twentieth century. 1" h. x 1.75" w. $75-95.

Vintage triple horse head pin with bridles and red accent, sterling, unmarked, c. 1930-40. 1.5" h. x 2.75" w. $70-90.

Lovely sterling silver horse head pin framed with circle, Beau, c. 1947-present. 1.5" dia. $65-80.

Detailed silver pony pendant surrounded by ring, c. early twentieth century. 1.5" dia. $110-145.

Race horse and jockey pin, white enameled horse colored paúe rhinestones throughout, unmarked, c. 1930-40. 1.75" h. x 2.5" w. $150-250.

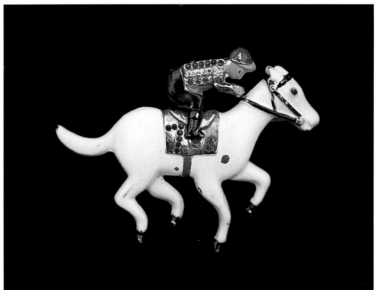

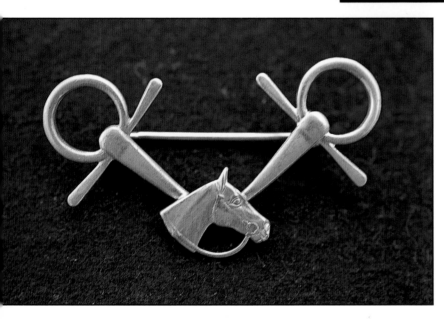

Golden stock pin with horse head mounted on snaffle bit, unmarked, c. early twentieth century. 1.25" h. x 1.75" w, $70-90.

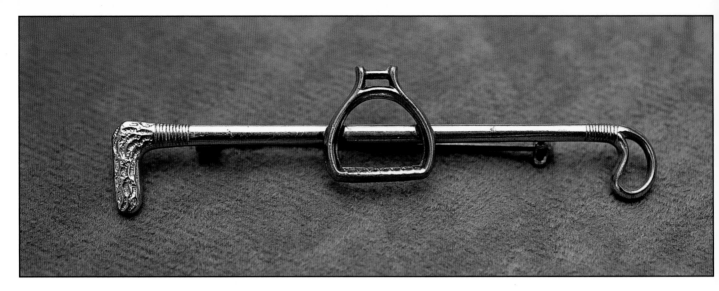

Nicely detailed combination gold and silver stock pin, stirrup set on riding crop, patented, c. 1936-37. 1" h. x 3" w. $60-85.

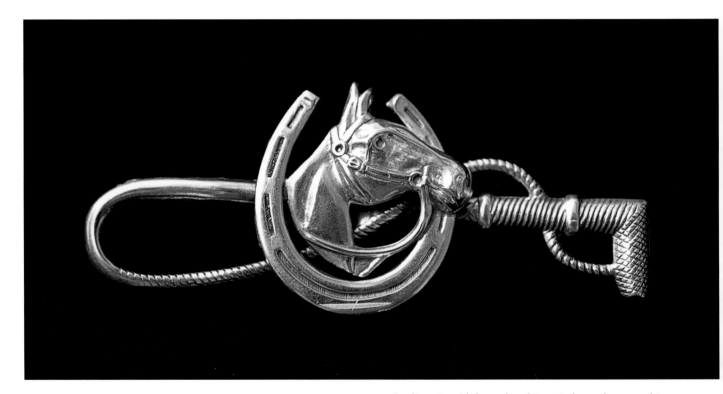

Sterling pin with horse head inset in horseshoe on whip, unmarked, c. 1930-40. 1" h. x 2.5" w. $60-85.

# *Victorian*

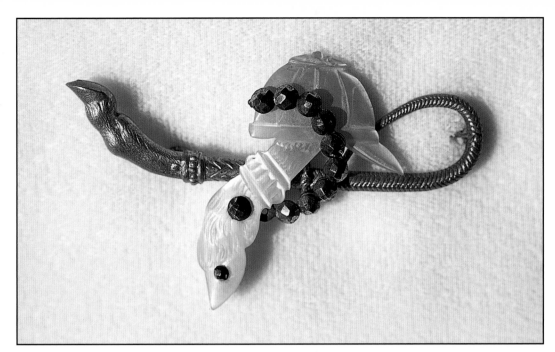

Stunning mother-of-pearl Victorian brooch with equestrian motif, mounted on golden hoofed crop, c. 1880-1910. 1.5" h. x 2.5" w. $225+.

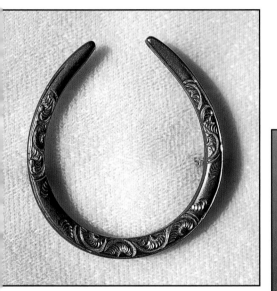

Gold-filled etched horseshoe pin, C-catch, unmarked, c. 1890-1910. 2.5" h. x 1.5" w. $90-125.

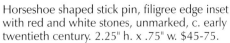

Unique metal buckle, Victorian design, Depose, Made in France, c. early to mid twentieth century. 1.25" h. x 2.25" w. $120-145.

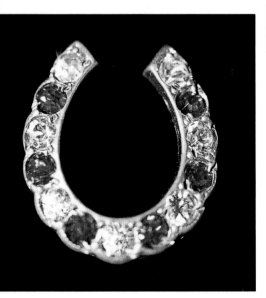

Horseshoe shaped stick pin, filigree edge inset with red and white stones, unmarked, c. early twentieth century. 2.25" h. x .75" w. $45-75.

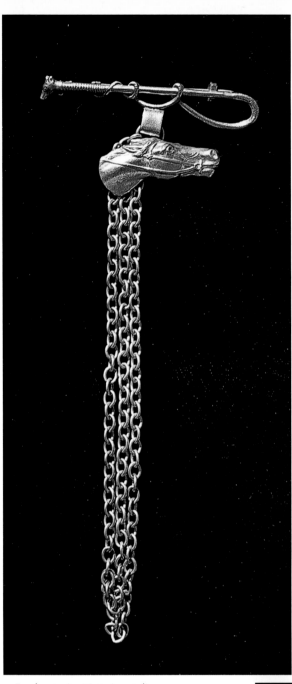

Celluloid pin marked F.C.B., with metal hanger of girl and horse marked Louisville, 1904. Pin and hanger stamped "The White-head & Hoag Co., Newark, NJ.," c. 1904. 3.5" h. x 1.5" w. $145-185.

Fox hunt pin, Victorian styling, stamped gold, c. 1890-1910. 7" h. x 2.75" w. $200+.

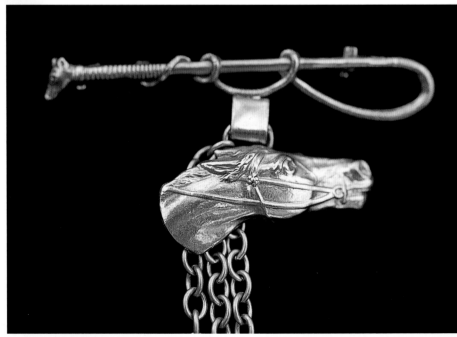

Detail of fox hunt pin.

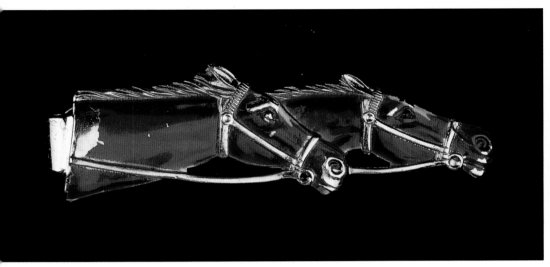

Horse head tie bar, enamel on base metal, Anson, Providence, Rhode Island, c. 1950. .75" h. x 2.25" w. $60-90.

Horse head cuff links, enamel on base metal, Anson, Providence, Rhode Island, c. 1950. .75" h. x 1.25" w. $55-85.

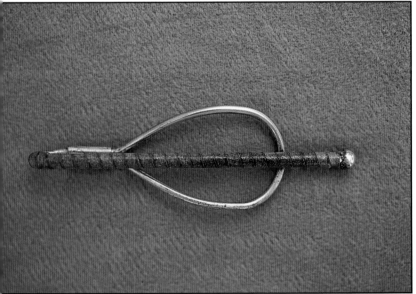

Riding crop tie clasp, leather bound, Swank, c. 1940. .75" h. x 2.5" w. $55-75.

Tie bar set, white mother-of-pearl with faux ruby eye, unmarked, c. 1950. Tie bar, .5" h. x 2" w. Cuff links, .5" h. x 1" w. $120-145.

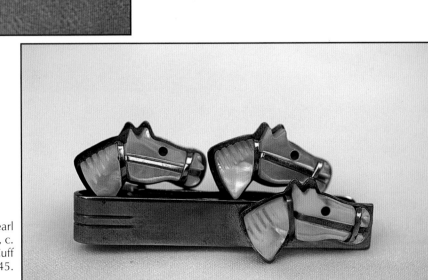

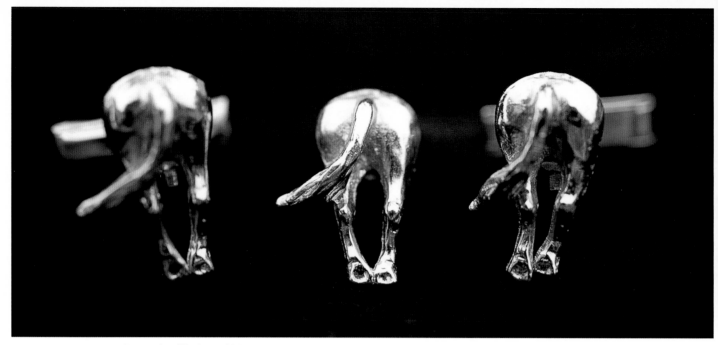

"Horse Power" tie bar and cuff links, gold horse's hind quarters, unmarked, c. 1960.
Tie bar, .75" h. x .5" w. Cuff links, .75" h. x .5" w. $50-75.

Elegant French enameled cuff links with steeplechase scene, Made in France, c. 1952-58. .75" h. x 1" w. $350+.

Detail of French enamel cuff links.

Majestic cuff links, gold horses with black etching and large center onyx, marked Swank, c. 1935. .75" h. x 1.25" w. $75-90.

Cuff links with gold-tone horse head surrounded by horseshoe, Kremen, c. 1940-1950. .75" h. x .75" w. $75-85.

Haras horse trainer cuff links, 24K gold plated, made from original buttons worn by grooms and stable hands, European, c. 1950. .85" dia. $55-75.

Fabulous wooden horse head pin with gold bridle, resembles Bakelite horse, C-catch, c. 1930. 3.25" h. x 2.25" w. $90-120.

Red thermoplastic horse head pin, nicely highlighted, C-catch, unmarked, c. 1930. 3.25" h. x 2.5" w. $30-50.

Red thermoplastic horse head pin attached to crop with unique handle, C-catch, signed, c. 1930. 1.5" h. x 2.5" w. $35-55.

Two-toned horse head metal money clip, Anson, Providence, Rhode Island, c. 1962. 1.75" dia. $45-70.

Stamped metal western horse pin, copper finish, unmarked, c. 1940-50. 2.25" h. x 2.5" w. $30-45.

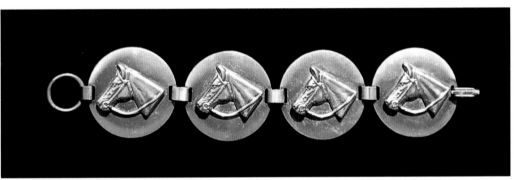

Four link copper bracelet, bridled horse head motif, unmarked, c. 1950. 1.5" h. x 7.75" w. $40-60.

Unique western belt buckle with moveable horse head in center that opens to insert coin, manufactured by Chambers Belt Co., c. mid twentieth century. 2.5" h. x 3.5" w. $60-80.

Back of buckle, showing chamber for coin.

Beautiful hand crafted sterling silver belt buckle, turquoise chip inlay with prancing white horse, Taxco, c. 1970. 2" h. x 3.5" w. $125-150.

Black and white Paint Horse set on tooled nickel silver buckle, signed, c. latter twentieth century. 2.5" h. x 3.75" w. $50-75.

# Chapter 9

# Awards—Ribbons, Medals, Trophies

"Riding turns 'I wish' into 'I can.'"
—Pam Brown (b. 1928)

Grouping of show awards featuring 1934 St. Louis trophy and an assortment of 1940 show ribbons from the Ohio region.

Detail of yellow and white pinback button, New London Horse Show, Plymouth Saddle Club, fourth prize, c. 1948. 15" h. x 6" w. $10-20.

Detail of pink pinback button, Boots and Saddle Horse Association, Bugyrus, Ohio, fifth prize, c. 1949. 14" h. x 4.75" w. $10-20.

Bombay Horse Show trophy, Arab stallion fourteen hands and under, sterling silver
J.D. & S., c. 1907. 5.25" h. x 2.5" dia. of cup. $175+.

Cortland County Fair Horse Show, blue
ribbon with pinback button, c. 1925.
10.25" h. x 4.75" w. $10-20.

*Center and above:* New York State Fair Horse Show,
Syracuse, New York, red ribbon with pinback button,
c. 1923. 9" h. x 4.75" w. $10-20.

Horse show trophy, sterling silver Kaag horse figure on marbleized base, c. mid twentieth century. 8.5" h. x 7.5" w. $60-85.

Cortland County Horse Fair, gold ribbon with pinback button, c. 1928. 11" h. x 4" w. $10-20.

St. Louis Spring Horse Show trophy, sterling silver, won by "Colonel Mac," c. 1934. 6.75" h. x 3.5" w. $90-125.

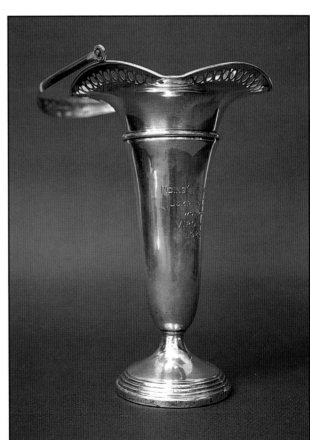

Riding and Hunt Club trophy, sterling silver basket with filigree basket and handle, c. 1928. 6.5" h. x 4.5" dia. of basket. $120-150.

The trio of horse show trophies from previous page.

Bronze horse show trophy, first place in five gaited class, c. 1943. 6" h. x 5" w. $60-90.

Western Illinois Fair trophy, brass and wood combination, horse manufactured by Dodge, U.S.A., c. 1954. 10" h. x 8" w. $75-95.

Gold plated medallion, The Saddle Horse Association of Philadelphia, manufactured by Augustus Frank and Company, Philadelphia, c. 1931. 1.5" dia. $25-40.

Bronze medallions, Philadelphia In-Door Horse Show, c. 1920. 1.5" dia. $30-50 each.

Detroit Horse Show medallion, silver plated, c. 1935. 1.5" dia. $25-40.

Magnificent silver trotting horse trophy, manufactured by H.M. Day, Hillsboro, Ohio, from Orchard Beach Racetrack, Scarboro, Maine, c. 1930. 7" h. x 8.5" w. $150-200.

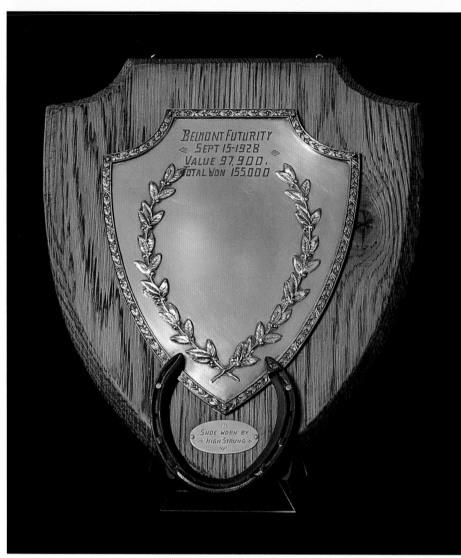

Unique wood and silver horse plaque, inscribed "Belmont Futurity, Sept. 15, 1928, Value $97,000, total won $155,000," rear shoe worn by "High Strung" mounted on bottom. Engraved silver plate on back reads: Wallace Brothers Company, Wallingford, Conn., V9742. 15" h. x 12.25" w. Value undetermined.

Detail of "High Strung" horseshoe.

# Chapter 10

# Art—Drawings, Prints, Ephemera

"The air of heaven is that which blows between a horse's ears."
—Arabian Proverb

Rendition of "Pharaoh's Horses," pastel on handmade paper. Framed in original handmade oval wooden frame with gesso carved rim, signed M. Kearsy, c. 1905. 20.5" dia. $975-1150.

Detail of "Pharaoh's Horses" pastel.

Chromolithograph of John F. Herring, "Pharaoh's Horses," original rope design frame, c. 1880. 17.5" h. x 22.75" w. $175-250.

Steel plate etching of John F. Herring, "Pharaoh's Horses," c. mid nineteenth century. 25.5" dia. $400+.

Detail of steel plate etching.

Print etching of John F. Herring "Pharaoh's Horses,"
in ornate double frame, c. 1900. 22" dia. $600+.

Hand colored, photo etched plate showing departure of horse drawn carriage from plantation celebration, c. 1855-60. 17" h. x 21" w. $525-850.

Sepia-toned postcard of "Horse Fair," by Rosa Bonheur, printed in England, c. 1907-15. 3.30" h. x 5.30" w. $8-12.

Horse Fair.

Rosa Bonheur.

Sepia-toned print of "A Norman Sire," by Rosa Bonheur, The Perry Pictures Company, Malden, Massachusetts, c. 1917. 8" h. x 5.5" w. $70-95.

Sepia-toned print of "A Noble Charger," by Rosa Bonheur, The Perry Pictures Company, Malden, Massachusetts, c. 1910. 8" h. x 5.5" w. $70-95.

Chromolithograph of "The Ford," by R. Atkinson Fox, in original frame, c. 1908. 12.75" h. x 14.5" w. $125-155.

Framed picture of George Stubbs, "A Grey Hack with a White Greyhound and Groom," printed in England, c. twentieth century. 6" h. x 8" w. $20-35.

Lithograph of Victorian lady riding sidesaddle, by Thomas Mitchell Pierce, Gray Lithograph Company, New York, c. 1908. 12.75" h. x 10" w. $50-75.

Wonderful color lithograph of woman with horse and dogs, c. 1950. 17" h. x 12" w. $50-70.

Embossed color lithograph of lady and horse, by Hy Hintermeister, c. 1940. 10" h. x 8" w. $40-65.

THE PRIZE WINNER

Color lithograph postcard "The Prize Winner," c. 1907-15. 3.5" h. x 5.5" w. $10-15.

Polo scene centerfold, England, c. 1880-95. 12.25" h. x 20.25" w. $175-225.

Pen and ink watercolor, by Maurice Taquoy, original frame, c. 1911. 14.25" h. x 25.25" w. $200+.

Detail of pen and ink watercolor.

Vintage framed fox hunt picture
with thermometer, marked Litho, in
U.S.A., c. mid twentieth century.
9.25" h. x 11.25" w. $35-55.

Set of four fox hunt color lithographs, copyright Sidney Z. Lucas, New York
City, c. 1940-50. 6" h. x 8" w. The four scenes illustrate departing for the
hunt, searching for the scent, the chase, and day's end. $70-90 set.

Vintage framed horse and rider silhouette under convex glass, c. 1940-50. 8.75" h. x 6.75" w. $50-75.

Framed silhouette picture, "The Hunt," Kaser, c. 1940. 8" h. x 11" w. $65-85.

Detail of "The Hunt" silhouette.

Detail of Victorian style German print, boy with pony, c. 1905. The full print (shown on page 1) measures 21" h. x 16" w. $70-95

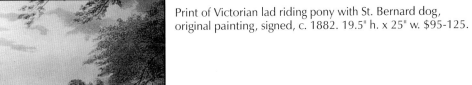

Print of Victorian lad riding pony with St. Bernard dog, original painting, signed, c. 1882. 19.5" h. x 25" w. $95-125.

Color lithograph of "First in the Race," Sackell & Wilhelms Litho Company, New York, New York, c. early twentieth century. 6.25" h. x 3.25" w. $25-45.

Black and white photo of boy with pony companions, from *National Geographic, World of Horses First Edition*, c. November, 1923. 10" h. x 7" w. $45-75.

Color lithograph of "Old Fashioned Friendship," by Hy Hintermeister, c. mid twentieth century. 14" h. x 11" w. $50-70.

Black and white photo of farmer with faithful horse, from *National Geographic, World of Horses First Edition*, c. November, 1923. 10" h. x 7" w. $45-75.

Framed color lithograph of "He Made the World a Better Place to Live In," A. Delia, c. 1937. 15" h. x 11" w. $60-85.

Framed print of lovely chestnut with white blaze, signed, c. 1950. 8.75" h. x 7.25" w. $35-55.

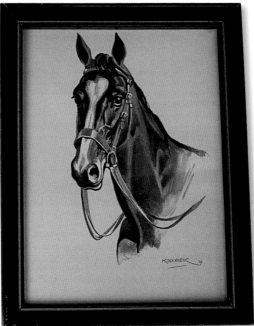

Nicely detailed pair of framed horse head prints, Koekkoek, copyright Donald Art Co. Inc., New York, New York, No. 412-413, c. 1939. 9" h. x 7" w. $70-90 pair.

Framed color portrait of bridled black
and gray horse heads, M. Gear, c. 1950.
9.75" h. x 7.75" w. $35-55.

Etching of "Greyhound" world champion
trotter, by R.H. Palenske, c. early twentieth
century. 16" h. x 12" w. $60-85.

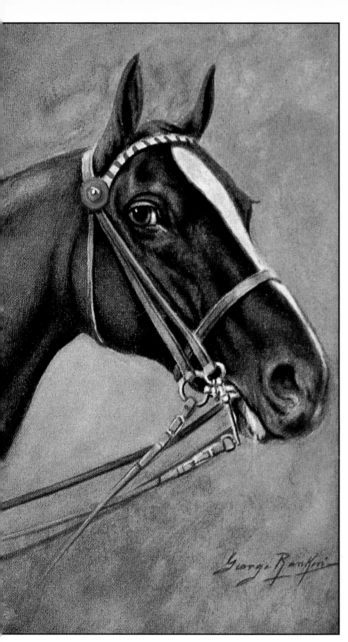

Horse head postcard, red rosette on bridle, by George Rankin, copyright, printed and published by J. Salmon Ltd., Seven Oaks, England, c. 1907-1915. 5.5" h. x 3.5" w. $10-15.

Color postcard of chestnut horse with yearning expression, by George Rankin, copyright, printed and published by J. Salmon Ltd., Seven Oaks, England, c. 1907-1915. 5.5" h. x 3.5" w. $10-15.

Framed photochrome postcard of Arlyne Clay up on Sidan, Scottsdale, Arizona, c. 1939-present. 6" h. x 8" w. $25-40.

Vintage, framed color print of cowgirl with palomino, c. 1940-50. 13" h. x 11" w. $40-60.

Photochrome postcard of Art Miller on Peavines Golden Major, c. 1939-present. 5.5" h. x 3.5" w. $8-10.

Color print of "The Palomino," by
Wesley Dennis, c. 1950. 12" h. x 15" w.
$15-25.

Humorous black and white print entitled "Calf
Roping," Cameron, c. 1949. 11" h. x 13.75" w. $35-55.

Linen postcard of rodeo cowboy,
"Crazy Snake up to one of his Tricks,"
c. 1920-50. 3.5" h. x 5.5" w. $10-15.

Black and white photo of a bronco-buster in action, from *National Geographic, World of Horses First Edition,* c. November, 1923. 10" h. x 7" w. $45-75.

Frank Van Meter Leaving Barrelhead

Linen postcard of rodeo cowboy, "Frank Van Meter Leaving Barrelhead," c. 1920-50. 3.5" h. x 5.5" w. $10-15.

# Chapter 11
# Author's Potpourri

"Of all animals kept for the recreation of mankind the horse is alone capable of exciting a passion that shall be absolutely hopeless."
—Bret Harte (1836-1902)

Robust brass horse head supported by marble pillar, unmarked, c. latter twentieth century. 14" h. x 8.25" w. $250+

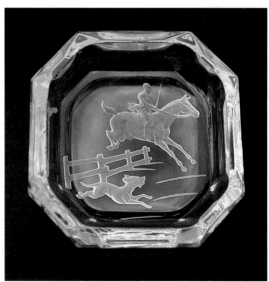

Clear crystal salt dish etched with rider jumping horse over fence, c. 1930-50. 2.4" h. x 2.3" w. $25-35.

Colorful Bakelite tray illustrated with carriage scene, Litholite, c. 1931-32. 7.25" h. x 12.25" w. $95-125.

Ivorine horse head bookends on marble base, intricately detailed, unmarked, c. 1950. 8.25" h. x 5.5" w. $225+.

Glass domed bridle rosettes of three horse heads on white background, H.A. Chapman, White Bear Lake, Minnesota, c. 1960. 1.75" dia. $65-95 for pair.

Glass domed bridle rosettes, pony express rider on white background, H.A. Chapman, White Bear Lake, Minnesota, c. 1960. 1.75" dia. $65-95 for pair.

Red glass domed bridle rosettes of eagle clutching flag displaying eighteen
stars, unmarked, c. nineteenth century. 1.75" dia. $195-250 for pair.

Brass calvary rosettes marked US, used on horse harnesses, leather saddle bags, and
other tack, c. 1861-1865 or earlier. 1.13" dia. $30-55 each.

Silver Victorian brush with boar bristles.
Eloquent horse head design resembles Rosa
Bonheur's "A Noble Charger," c. 1890-1910.
4.5" h. x 3" w. $200+.

Pair of Bakelite tortoise shell buttons adorned
with gold horse heads. Design similar to Rosa
Bonheur's "A Noble Charger," c. early
twentieth century. 2" dia. $50-70 each.

Polo player place card stands, enamel on brass base, hallmark, France, c. 1930. 1.5" h. x .75" w. $125+ set.

Elegant three piece white porcelain tobacciana set, Evans, c. mid twentieth century. Table lighter, 7" h. x 4.75" w. Ashtray, 5.5" dia. Container, 2.5" h. x 2.75" base. $85-125 set.

Left: Bone handle riding crop with sterling silver band, wood shaft, and leather popper, c. late nineteenth/early twentieth century. 31" l. $200-250. Right: Victorian riding crop, ivory handle with etched silver overlay, featuring horse head, horseshoes, and stirrups, c. latter nineteenth century. 26.5" l. Value undetermined.

From left: Old English cork and leather hip flask, cork stopper with Victorian hallmark, Chester, England, c. mid nineteenth century. 6" h. x 2.5" w.; porcelain match holder mounted on leather covered metal box, featuring dressage rider in Piaffe movement, unmarked, c. 1930-50. 2.5" h. x 1.75" w.; 1894 *Pipe and Pouch, The Smokers Own Book of Poetry*; antique hip flask, leather upper with metal base and cap, Nimrod, c. early twentieth century. 6" h. x 3.25" w. Value undetermined.

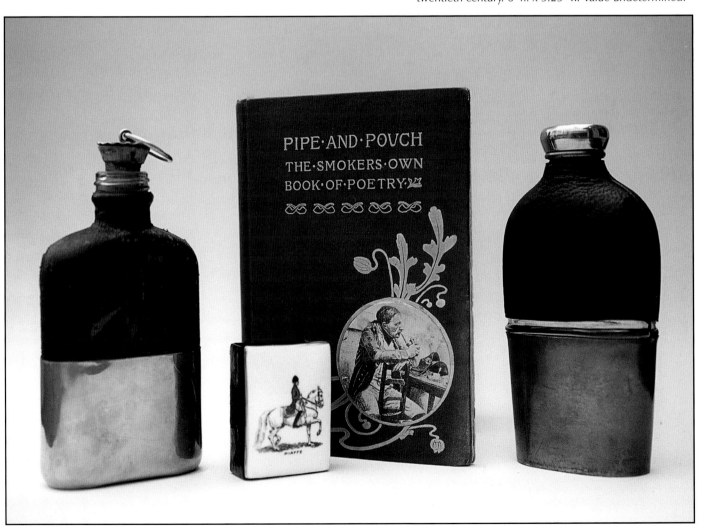

# The Horse Prayer

*To thee, My Master, I offer my prayer.*

*Feed me, water and care for me, and, when the day's work is done, provide me with shelter, a clean dry bed and a stall wide enough for me to lie down in comfort. Always be kind to me. Talk to me. Do not jerk the reins, and do not whip me when going up hill. Pet me sometimes, that I may serve you the more gladly and learn to love you. Never strike, beat or kick me when I do not understand what you want, but give me a chance to understand you. Watch me, and if I fail to do your bidding, see if something is wrong with my harness or feet. Do not check me so that I cannot have the free use of my head. If you insist that I wear blinders, so that I cannot see behind me as it was intended I should, I pray you be careful that the blinders stand well out from my eyes. Do not overload me, or hitch me where water will drip on me. Keep me well shod. Examine my teeth when I do not eat. I may have an ulcerated tooth, and that, you know is very painful. Do not tie my head in an unnatural position, or take my best defense against flies and mosquitoes by cutting off my tail. I can not tell you in words when I am thirsty, so give me clean cool water often. Save me, by all means in your power, from that fatal disease — the glandeers. I cannot tell you in words when I am sick, so watch me, that by signs you may know my condition. Give me all possible shelter from the hot sun, and put a blanket on me, not when I am working, but when I am standing in the cold. Never put a cold bit in my mouth; first warm it by holding it in your hand for a moment. I try to carry you and your burdens without a murmur and wait patiently for you long hours of the day or night. Without the power to choose my shoes or path I sometimes fall on hard pavements which I have often prayed might be of wood but of such a nature as to give me a safe and sure footing. Remember that I must be ready at any moment to lose my life in your service. And finally, O My Master, when my useful strength is gone, do not turn me out to starve or freeze, or sell me to some cruel owner, to be slowly tortured and starved to death; but do thou, My Master, take my life in the kindest way, and your God will reward you here and hereafter. You will not consider me irreverent if I ask this in the name of Him who was born in a stable.*

"The Horse Prayer," anonymous. Date unknown, although the disease "glandeers" prevailed in Europe from the seventeenth through nineteenth centuries. 12" h. x 9.5" w. $20-35.

Illustration from *Sportsman's Sketchbook*, by Lionel Edwards RI, "Old Mare and Three Days Old Foal."

# Bibliography

Bagdade, Susan, and Al Bagdade. *Warman's American Pottery and Porcelain.* Radnor, Pennsylvania: Wallace-Homestead, 1994.

Bagdade, Susan, and Al Bagdade. *Warman's English and Continental Pottery and Porcelain: Third Edition.* Iola, Wisconsin: Krause Publications, 1998.

Biggle, Jacob. *Biggle Horse Book.* Philadelphia, Pennsylvania: Wilmer Atkinson Company, 1913.

Congdon-Martin, Douglas. *Figurative Cast Iron: A Collector's Guide.* Atglen, Pennsylvania: Schiffer Publishing, Ltd., 1994.

Exley, Helen. *Horse Quotations.* Mount Kisco, New York: Exley Giftbooks, 1993.

Florence, Gene. *The Collector's Encyclopedia of Occupied Japan Collectibles. Fifth Series.* Paducah, Kentucky: Collector Books, 1992.

Giacomini, Mary Jane. *American Bisque: A Collector's Guide With Prices.* Atglen, Pennsylvania: Schiffer Publishing, Ltd., 1994.

Gibbs, Carl Jr. *Collector's Encyclopedia of Metlox Potteries: Identification and Values.* Paducah, Kentucky: Collector Books, 1995.

Grizel, Ruth Ann. *American Slag Glass: Identification and Values.* Paducah, Kentucky: Collector Books, 1998.

Huxford, Sharon, and Bob Huxford. *The Collector's Encyclopedia of Brush-McCoy Pottery.* Paducah, Kentucky: Collector Books, 1996.

Kerins, Jack, and Elynore Kerins. *Collecting Antique Stickpins: Identification and Value Guide.* Paducah, Kentucky: Collector Books, 1995.

Kovel, Ralph, and Terry Kovel. *Dictionary of Marks: Pottery and Porcelain.* New York, New York: Crown Publishing, Inc., 1953.

Kovel, Ralph, and Terry Kovel. *Kovels' Antiques and Collectibles: Price List 2000.* New York, New York: Three Rivers Press, 2000.

Kovel, Ralph, and Terry Kovel. *Kovels' New Dictionary of Marks.* New York, New York: Crown Publishers, Inc., 1986.

Kowalsky, Arnold A., and Dorothy E. Kowalsky. *Encyclopedia of Marks on American, English and European Earthenware, Ironstone, and Stoneware, 1780-1980.* Atglen, Pennsylvania: Schiffer Publishing, Ltd., 1999.

Kuritzky, Louis. *Collector's Guide to Bookends: Identification and Values.* Paducah, Kentucky: Collector Books, 1998.

Lehner, Lois. *Lehner's Encyclopedia of U.S. Marks on Pottery, Porcelain and Clay.* Paducah, Kentucky: Collector Books, 1988.

MacDonald-Taylor, Margaret. *A Dictionary of Marks.* London, England: Barrie and Jenkins, Ltd., 1992.

Mangus, Jim, and Bev Mangus. *Shawnee Pottery: An Identification and Value Guide.* Paducah, Kentucky: Collector Books, 1994.

McBride, Gerald P. *A Collector's Guide to Cast Metal Bookends: With Values.* Atglen, Pennsylvania: Schiffer Publishing, Ltd., 1997.

McCarthy, Ruth. *More Lefton China.* Atglen, Pennsylvania: Schiffer Publishing, Ltd., 2000.

McCaslin, Mary J. *Royal Bayreuth: A Collector's Guide.* Marietta, Ohio: Antique Publications, 1994.

Newbound, Betty, and Bill Newbound. *Collector's Encyclopedia of Figural Planters and Vases: Identification and Values.* Paducah, Kentucky: Collector Books, 1997.

Peterson, Arthur G. *400 Trademarks on Glass.* Gas City, Indiana: L-W Book Sales, 1968.

Röntgen, Robert E. *Marks on German, Bohemian and Austrian Porcelain, 1710 to the Present. Updated and Revised Edition.* Atglen, Pennsylvania: Schiffer Publishing, Ltd., 1997.

Sanders, W. Eugene Jr., and Christine C. Sanders. *Pocket Matchsafes: Reflections of Life and Art, 1840-1920.* Atglen, Pennsylvania: Schiffer Publishing, Ltd., 1997.

Santiso, Tom. *TV Lamps: Identification and Value Guide.* Paducah, Kentucky: Collector Books, 1999.

Schneider, Mike. *Grindley Pottery: A Menagerie.* Atglen, Pennsylvania: Schiffer Publishing, Ltd., 1996.

Schneider, Mike. *Royal Copley: Identification and Price Guide.* Atglen, Pennsylvania: Schiffer Publishing, Ltd., 1995.

Seecof, Robert, Donna Seecof, and Louis Kuritzky. *Bookend Revue.* Atglen, Pennsylvania: Schiffer Publishing, Ltd., 1996.

Shepherd, Calvin. *50s T.V. Lamps.* Atglen, Pennsylvania: Schiffer Publishing, Ltd., 1998.

White, Carole Bess. *Collector's Guide to Made in Japan Ceramics: Identification and Values.* Paducah, Kentucky: Collector Books, 1994.

Wolfe, Leslie C., and Marjorie A. Wolfe. *Royal Copley: Plus Royal Windsor and Spaulding.* Paducah, Kentucky: Collector Books, 1992.

# Index

# About the Author

Deborah Rashkin is both a horsewoman and avid collector. Born in Canada, she now resides in both Tempe, Arizona and Durango, Colorado. An accredited paralegal and proprietor of Horsetiques (www.Horsetiques.com), she specializes in antiques and collectibles relating to horses. At home, her barn encompasses a variety of breeds ranging from European Warmbloods to a Miniature Horse. Deborah's love and admiration of horses began at an early age. Today she respects and appreciates all aspects of horsemanship with a particular focus on the study of Dressage.

Deborah and her Jack Russell Terrier, "Sugar."

"Rosie," Painted Miniature Horse.

"Notorius," Anglo Trakehner mare.

"Capernious," Holsteiner colt.

"Rhapsody," Dutch Warmblood filly.